MARY GOSTELOW'S
Book of
EMBROIDERY
PROJECTS

MARY GOSTELOW'S
Book of
EMBROIDERY
PROJECTS

with photographs by Martin Gostelow

David & Charles
Newton Abbot   London   North Pomfret (Vt)

Photographs by Martin Gostelow

Library of Congress Catalog Card Number

British Library Cataloguing in Publication Data

Gostelow, Mary
    Mary Gostelow's book of embroidery projects
    1. Embroidery – Patterns
    I. Book of embroidery projects
    746.4'4   TT771
    ISBN 0-7153-7890-2

Typeset by ABM Typographics Ltd, Hull
Printed in Great Britain
by Redwood Burn Ltd, Trowbridge & Esher
for David & Charles (Publishers) Limited
Brunel House Newton Abbot Devon

Published in the United States of America
by David & Charles Inc
North Pomfret   Vermont 05053   USA

Contents

Introduction		7
Mary Gostelow's basic survival embroidery basket		9
1	Apply a pair of puppets	11
2	Assisi bag	19
3	Bargello typewriter cover	22
4	Blackwork 'special clutch'	26
5	Broderie anglaise housecoat	31
6	Cards for all occasions	35
7	Chainstitched games boards	39
8	Couch a little box	43
9	Crewel mirror surround	47
10	Cross stitch sampler trio	51
11	Pattern darn a skirt	61
12	Design an 'art' needlepoint	63
13	. . . and make it up	69
14	Drawn thread tie	72
15	Hardanger tray	75
16	Hedebo sun visor	78
17	Knot-initialled tennis dress	83
18	Machine-stitched blanket cover	90
19	Metallic kaftan	93
20	Needlepaint your 'home town'	97
21	Needlepoint tops for all the family	99
22	Net curtain with a difference	105
23	Patchwork jacket	107
24	Pulled thread tissue cover	112
25	Quilt your camera case	116
26	Raisedwork miniature	119
27	Sample 'family tree'	126
28	Shadow-work pincushion	131
29	Smock a family heirloom	134
30	White wedding dress	139
Main stitches		143
Suppliers		147
Acknowledgements		148
Index		149

Introduction

Many of the projects in this book are practical. Some you can wear; others can decorate your house. There are projects for gifts and designs that are intended purely to be decorative. I hope there is something for everyone.

You will find that all projects are marked with *asterisks*, which refer to dexterity as well as to stitching experience. Projects with one * are, to my mind, the easiest. At the end of every project are ideas for adaptations or related needleworks. Complete making up instructions are given.

As far as possible I have worked with inexpensive materials, because I feel strongly that embroidery should not be exclusive. I have tried to use machine-washable and easily available fabrics. Many projects require a minimum of expensive thread.

What is needed
All special materials and requirements are listed with each project. You probably already have to hand what I call my 'basic embroidery survival kit', consisting of 2 pairs of scissors, pins and needles. I have designed a practical basket to hold these items and you can find full instructions below. You will also constantly need the 'often wanteds':

> Tube turner for turning narrow tubes right side out
> Frames and hoops (I most often work with lightweight Abelcraft hoops, 10 and 20cm diameter sizes: these are excellent for all except canvas projects, which require a rectangular or square frame)
> Ruler and selection of soft pencils and eraser
> NEPO pen (an excellent non-run marker, particularly good on canvas)
> 'Invisible' pen for temporary markings: this produces a detergent-like blue line which washes out on contact with cold water. It should not be used for canvas and is most recommended for temporary markings on white cottons
> Tracing paper and dressmaker's carbon for transposing designs
> Iron
> Sewing machine
> Large sheets of paper for enlarging paper patterns

Pattern scales and stitches
Many patterns are actual size. To enlarge a pattern, draw out squares of the specified size on a large sheet of paper. Each of your squares corresponds to a small square on the printed pattern. Draw the pattern on your squared paper accordingly. Measurements are given as height × width.

Always 'strip' stranded cottons: cut a length and pull out strands one by one. Put together as many strands as you need. This gives a smoother, silkier finish. Stitches are shown in the relevant chapter or at the end of the book. Use the index. If you feel inspired to try more complicated embroidery forms, there are lots of ideas in my handbook, *The Coats Book of Embroidery*, which you will see I mention quite often as a source of more detailed information.

My 'basic survival embroidery kit' includes dressmaking and fine-pointed scissors (both by Fiskars, manufactured under licence by Wilkinson Sword), rustless lace pins and a selection of needles (full instructions are given for making the basket cover).

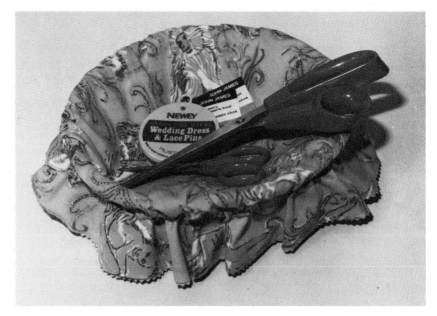

A list of 'often wanteds' includes lightweight hoops (both by Abelcraft), a long and slender tube turner, a NEPO indelible marker and a white-cased blue 'ink' invisible pen for temporary markings.

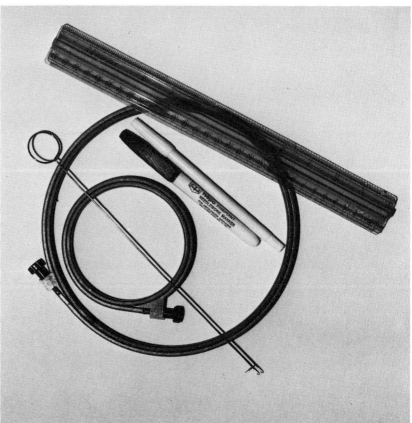

Mary Gostelow's basic survival embroidery basket *

Simplicity is the keynote of my organisation. I have tried out complicated needlework boxes and at one time I made myself a basket fitted with numerous little pockets. The only trouble was that I could not remember what went in which pocket and I wasted a lot of time trying to find things.

I have therefore designed this basket with no pockets so that all the contents are instantly visible. Similarly I made the cover in a bright turquoise and yellow monkey design to contrast with the orange handles of my scissors. The cover is double-sided and is held on to the basket with a large elastic circle, so that it can easily be taken off for machine-washing.

You can adapt the following 'recipe' to any size of basket but directions here are given for a round basket, 23cm diameter.

To make an embroidery basket you will need

    45cm of 90cm wide fabric to form a cover for a 23cm diameter
    basket (I used an all-cotton dress fabric)
    All-purpose thread to match
    76cm elastic, 5mm wide
    Ruler
    Large bodkin
    Pencil
    Pinking shears
    Basket; it must have a noticeable rim
    And if you are not working on a sewing machine you will need a
    pointed needle, say a sharp 8

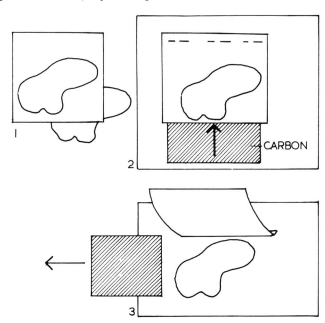

Tracing paper and carbon method of transposition: make a tracing of the printed design (1) and pin the paper, along one side only, to the fabric. Insert the carbon paper, carbon side down (2). Go over the traced outline firmly. Do not remove the pinned tracing paper until you have removed the carbon paper to check exactly whether all the design has gone through to the fabric (3).

To cut out 2 circles of fabric, fold the entire area in half (1) and half again (2) and again (3). You can then, with a ruler swinging from point A, mark a few circumferential points (4). Cut along this circumferential line, through all 8 layers of fabric at once, and you have 2 complete circles.

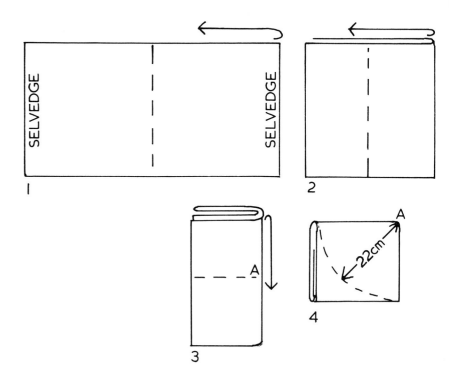

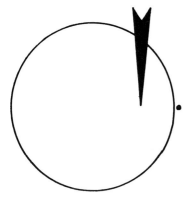

An easy way to sew an exact circle! In this case place the fabric under the machine foot (large arrow) so that it is 5cm from the edge of the fabric. Mark on the machine exactly where that edge is (dot). Start stitching, concentrating on the dot and the fact that the edge of the fabric reaches it, and you will sew an exact circle.

First fold your fabric in half as shown, then in half again and half again. On the area facing you, measure radii for a circle 22cm radius. Cut through all layers of fabric along this circle line and open up – you should now have 2 complete circles.

Lay these circles together right sides out, pin and stitch 3mm in around the circumference. Now place the fabrics in the machine so that you are going to start stitching 5cm in: make a note where the edge of the fabric lies on your sewing machine and, keeping the edge always at that point, start stitching – you will find you now stitch another complete circle 5cm in from the circumference. Similarly work a third line of stitching set in 6.5cm from the circumference.

Pink all round the circumference, close to but not through the outermost stitching. Make a tiny hole somewhere in the channel (between the 5 and 6.5cm stitchings) and pass the bodkin threaded with the elastic through the channel. Tie the ends neatly, turn the cover other side up, and fit the elastic over the basket's rim.

Other ideas for this basket concept

If you are using a handled basket, follow the above directions, but when you have done all the stitched circles make 2 slits from the circumference in to the inside of the channel. Place the cover on the basket and then thread the elastic through, outside the handles.
Why not cover another basket – to hold rolls and beads at table? And another – larger! – to hold baby or his or her things?

1 Apply a pair of puppets **

Glove puppets can occupy children – and others – for many an hour and I designed a schoolboy puppet for my nephew Joshua May and a feminine puppet for his little sister Olivia.

Both puppets are felt-decorated with appliqué which, as you can read more fully in my embroidery book, generally means one material applied on to or under another. The schoolboy is basically bright scarlet; he wears a yellow school cap, a brown and yellow tie and in his breast pocket is a handkerchief with his initial. The girl puppet is a pale purple. She has black woollen plaits and a black fringe. She wears an apron with her name on it, and underneath her gathered skirt is a little pocket for her green handkerchief.

You can of course use your own scraps of felt and small amounts of corresponding DMC stranded cottons to make differently coloured puppets, or you may buy materials to make them in my colour schemes.

A happy partnership: schoolboy and schoolgirl glove puppets, 30cm high.

To make the boy puppet you will need

> 2 areas of bright red felt each 30 × 30cm
> Other colours of felt, 20 × 20cm squares, beige, brown, yellow
> 1 skein each DMC stranded cotton 321 red, 973 yellow,
> 842 beige and 433 brown
> Pointed needle (say crewel 8)
> Tracing paper and carbon

Using the tracing paper and carbon method explained on p 9, cut out felt shapes. You should have:

red – 2 main bodies, 1 pocket
beige – 4 hand shapes, 2 eyes, 1 handkerchief
brown – 2 tie pieces
yellow – 3 hat crowns, 1 peak.

Body front

Following the marked outlines on 1 of your body shapes, apply the 2 eyes. Place 1 eye shape within an outline, pin it in place and hem around its edge with 1 strand of beige thread. Apply the other eye. Place a beige hand on top of each red hand area and hem AB. Apply the pocket with 1 strand of red thread. Chainstitch the mouth outline with 3 strands of brown.

Body back and joining

Apply the other 2 hand shapes to the relevant areas with beige hemming. Place the front and back of the body together, right sides out, and buttonhole stitch all around – sides, arms and hands and head – so that only the base of the puppet is open.

Now you are ready for the *finishing touches*. Chainstitch your required initial (pencil it in lightly first) in one corner of the handkerchief, fold it and put it in the pocket. Join the 2 tie pieces together AB with 1 strand of brown. Chainstitch yellow stripes on the tie with 3 strands of yellow thread. Join together, with 2 strands of yellow buttonhole stitch, the 3 crown pieces of the cap along AB lines and similarly attach the straight side of the peak to part of the base of the cap.

To make the girl puppet you will need

> 2 areas of pale purple felt each 30 × 30cm
> Other colours of felt, 20 × 20cm squares, black, darker purple, lime green
> 1oz thick black wool (knitting wool or, say, DMC Floralia noir)
> 1 skein each DMC stranded cotton 552 purple, 973 yellow,
> 310 black, 3348 green
> Pointed needle (say crewel 8)
> Tracing paper and carbon

Cut out the following felt shapes:

pale purple – 2 main bodies (1 with eyes and mouth cut out)
green – 4 hand pieces, 1 large face piece, 1 handkerchief
dark purple – 1 apron yoke, 1 apron skirt
black – 1 fringe, 1 pocket

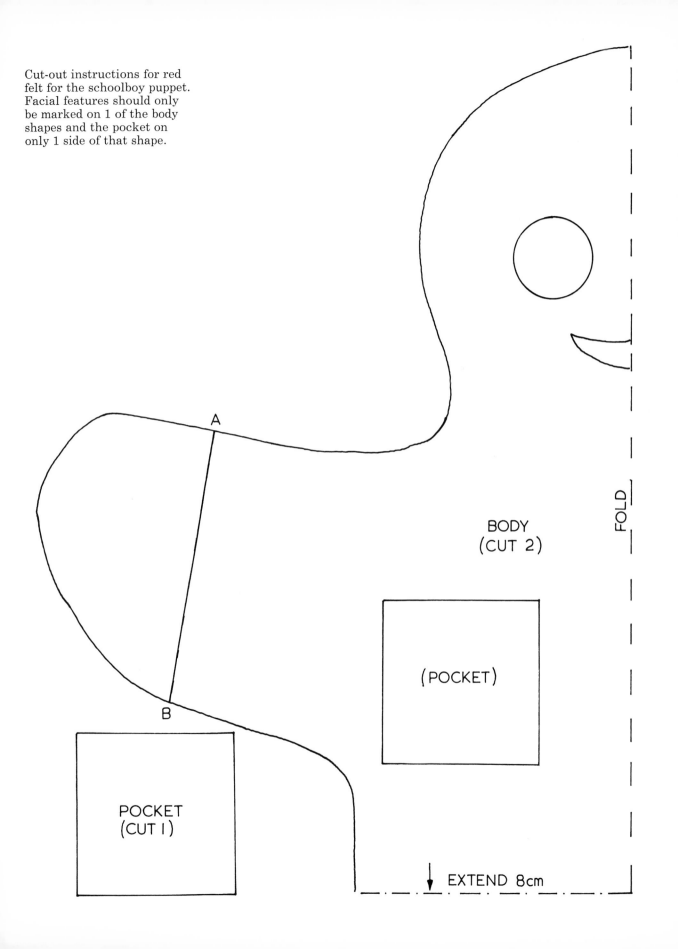

Cut-out instructions for red felt for the schoolboy puppet. Facial features should only be marked on 1 of the body shapes and the pocket on only 1 side of that shape.

A

B

FOLD

BODY
(CUT 2)

(POCKET)

POCKET
(CUT 1)

EXTEND 8cm

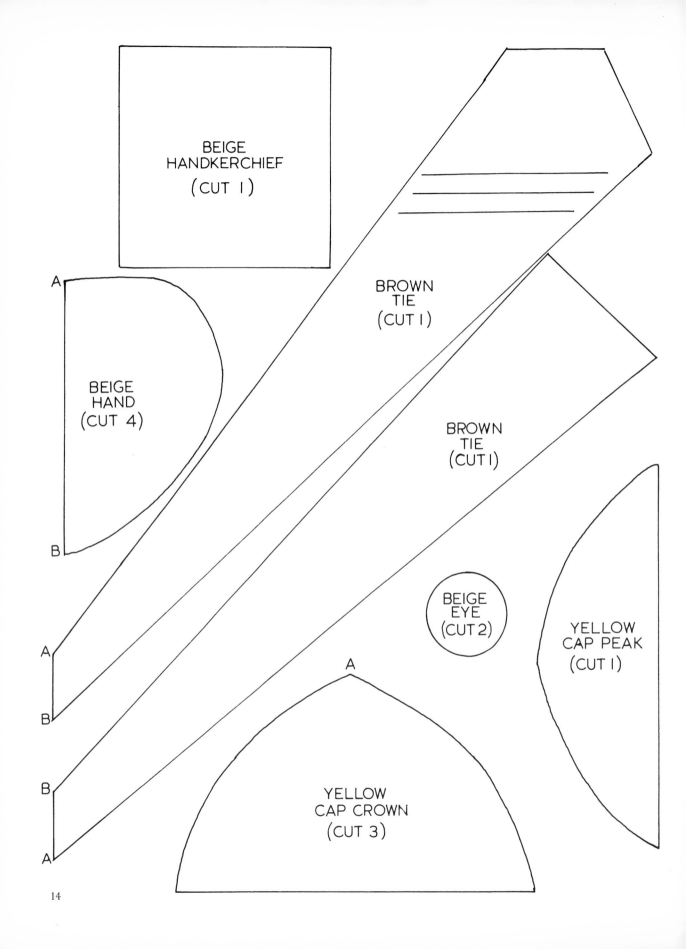

BEIGE
HANDKERCHIEF
(CUT 1)

BROWN
TIE
(CUT 1)

BROWN
TIE
(CUT 1)

BEIGE
HAND
(CUT 4)

A
B

A
B

B
A

BEIGE
EYE
(CUT 2)

YELLOW
CAP PEAK
(CUT 1)

A

YELLOW
CAP CROWN
(CUT 3)

14

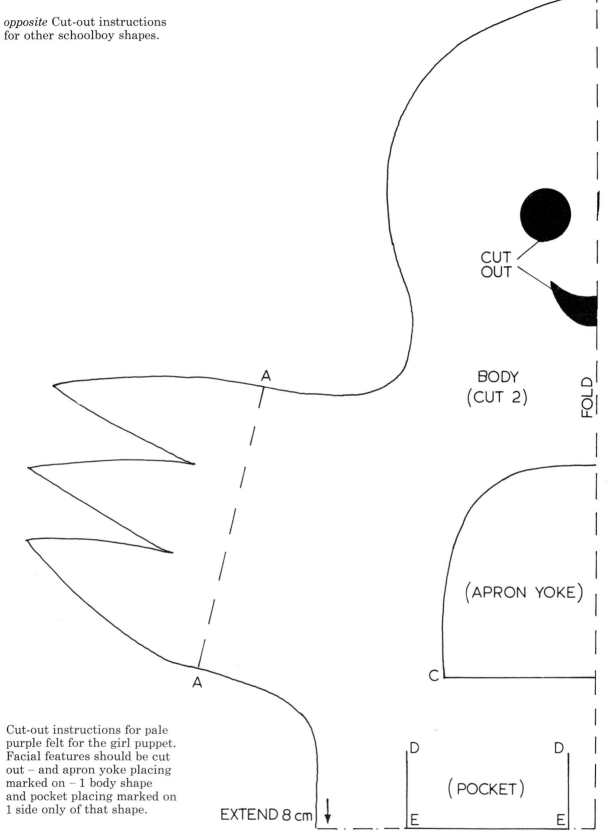

opposite Cut-out instructions for other schoolboy shapes.

CUT OUT

BODY (CUT 2)

FOLD

A

(APRON YOKE)

C

A

Cut-out instructions for pale purple felt for the girl puppet. Facial features should be cut out – and apron yoke placing marked on – 1 body shape and pocket placing marked on 1 side only of that shape.

EXTEND 8 cm ↓

D   D

(POCKET)

E   E

15

opposite Cut-out instructions for other girl shapes.

Body front

You are going to attach the facial features and hands with underlay appliqué, a variation on the more usual form of 'add on' appliqué. First lay the green 'face' piece underneath the cut-out features. Pin the green piece from the front of the purple felt. Hem the purple felt to the green felt with 1 strand of purple thread. Place a green hand shape under the purple zigzags of sleeve so that AB match and work running stitch (1 strand purple) AB through both felts. Attach the other green hand to the other purple sleeve.

Some of the *finishing touches* should be worked now. Fold the pocket shape EE and place it on the marked front body. Hem the pocket DE and DE, making sure that you stitch through both layers of black and purple felts, with 1 strand black thread. Pencil the required name on the apron yoke and stitch it in 3 strands yellow chainstitch: use 3 strands yellow thread for individual chainstitch flower petals and french knots for the flowers on the apron skirt. Work long running stitches (1 strand purple) along the top of the apron skirt AB.

Pin the apron yoke on to the body and hem all around with 1 strand of purple. Pull the long running stitches in the apron skirt so that the skirt fits CC on the apron yoke. Pin skirt in place, hem CC to body.

Body back and joining

Attach the 2 green hand shapes under the pink sleeves as before. Now lay the 2 body shapes together, right sides out, and buttonhole stitch all around so that only the base of the puppet is open. Switch from 1 strand purple to 1 strand green thread when you stitch the hand shapes (the pink sleeves should be loose from the running stitches).

Hair and other finishing touches

Place the fringe in position on the front of the head and buttonhole stitch the curved side to the head, 1 strand black thread. Now turn the puppet over and lay lengths of black wool, 20cm long, one by one vertically on the back of the head so that 2cm of each wool extends above the head. Attach each wool with a small back stitch (1 strand black thread) through to the buttonholing of the fringe. When you have covered the whole of the back of the head with vertical wool like this, work little running stitches (1 strand black) from one side of the head to the other, about halfway down the head,

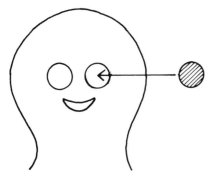

A felt eye shape is 'applied', in this case put on top of the marked area of the body front and subsequently held with hemming round the edge.

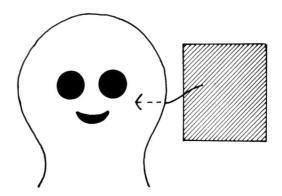

For this underlay appliqué, the green 'facial features' shape (shaded here) is placed beneath the cut-out eyes and mouth. The purple felt is then hemmed to the green.

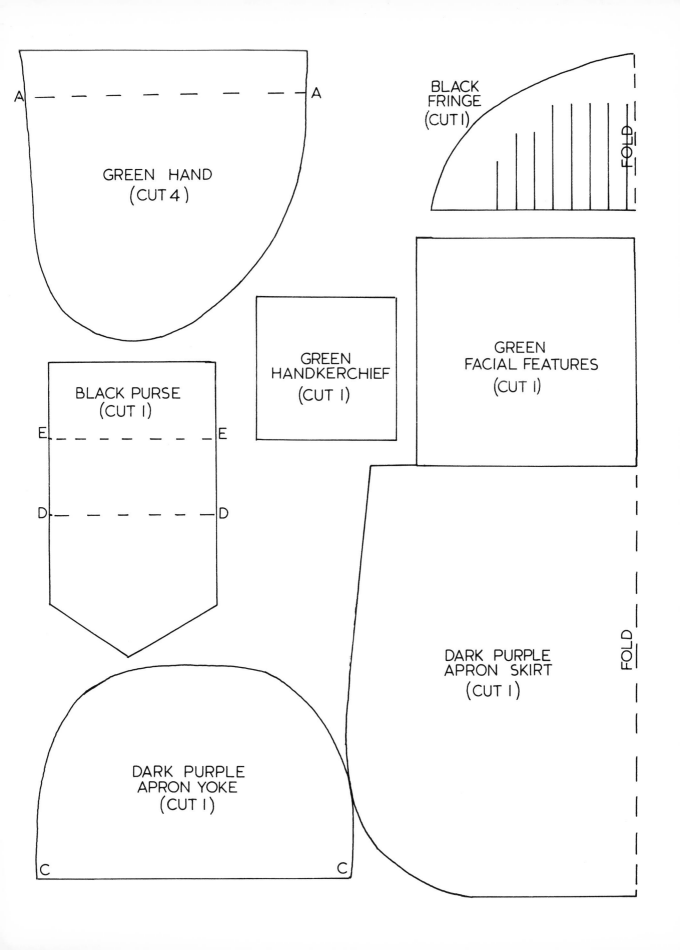

A———————————A

GREEN HAND
(CUT 4)

BLACK
FRINGE
(CUT 1)

FOLD

BLACK PURSE
(CUT 1)

E—————————E

D—————————D

GREEN
HANDKERCHIEF
(CUT 1)

GREEN
FACIAL FEATURES
(CUT 1)

DARK PURPLE
APRON SKIRT
(CUT 1)

FOLD

DARK PURPLE
APRON YOKE
(CUT 1)

C   C

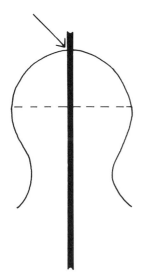

To form the main hair, a 20cm black wool length is laid vertically on the back body, protruding 2cm above the head. A small back stitch placed at the arrow holds the wool to the head (later, when all the back of the head is covered in this way with vertically-laid wool lengths, running stitches will be worked horizontally across the head, as indicated by the dotted line).

making sure that you 'catch' each of the wool threads on the way (to avoid sewing through to the front of the head with this stitching you might find it easier to hold your other hand in the puppet as you stitch).

Lift up the girl's apron skirt, put in her little green handkerchief (which you can initial if you like), plait her hair and tie with yellow thread – and she is ready to play with her schoolboy companion.

Other ideas relating to this project

Use a 'front shape' worked according to the above instructions and embellished with her name to decorate a girl's nightdress case.

Adapt the patterns here to produce a whole family of puppets, named for each member of *your* family.

Alternatively, adapt the puppets to produce a Punch and Judy cast.

2 Assisi bag **

Are you like me? Do you value especially gifts that someone has taken the time and trouble to make? Do you in turn enjoy the planning and work that goes into making such a gift for a dear friend?

I decided to work a little bag for a young friend who is tall and slim and often carries a shoulder purse. It is informal enough for daytime wear. With a plain black dress or pantsuit it would look stunning for a bistro evening.

My bag is made of Glenshee evenweave linen lined with bright orange felt. It has 1 long gusset that is joined to the sides and the base of the front and back panels. The front panel is worked in Assisi style in bright orange and black stranded cottons.

You can read about Assisi work on p 22ff of *The Coats Book of Embroidery*. It is fun to stitch and effective when it is finished!

My main motif is a seahorse, copied from a design by the 16th century artist Conrad Gesner and published in his *Nomenclator aquatilium animantium* . . . (Zurich 1560, p 267). It can be found in Dover's republication *Curious Woodcuts of Fanciful and Real Beasts* (1971, p 92).

To make this bag you will need

    50 cm Glenshee evenweave linen, ivory, 132cm wide (you can
    use any similar evenweave fabric)
    Orange felt, to match colour of embroidery thread, 35 × 60cm
    All-purpose sewing thread, colour of linen
    1 skein each DMC stranded cotton 310 black, 970 orange
    24 tapestry needle
    Tracing paper
    Dressmaker's carbon

First cut out linen shapes as illustrated. You will need 2 pieces, 1 each for the back and front, 1 length 5cm wide for the gusset and 1 length 9cm wide for the handle. Temporarily bind the edges of what will be the front panel of the bag with tape or stitches. You can use tracing paper and dressmaker's carbon to put the design in the centre of this panel. Change the initials I have used ('ETC') to suit: you can copy those you want from the lettering illustrated on p 89.

Assisi does not have to be worked with a frame. All your stitching will be in *2 strands* of stranded cotton, stripped and put together, *over 2 threads* of fabric. First work the outline of the seahorse in back or double-running stitches, making sure that all your stitches are *over 2 threads* of fabric and either vertical, horizontal or exactly diagonal.

Now you fill in all the 'reserves' of the design, the area around the seahorse, in orange cross stitches *over 2 threads* of fabric. Make sure that all your upper diagonals face the same way. And remember that your stitching should not pierce or cover the seahorse outline.

When all the cross stitching is finished, the 2 outer border lines

This teenager's shoulder bag would look good on the beach or at a disco! The seahorse panel in Assisi style measures 25 × 15 cm. The off-white linen bag is lined with bright orange felt to match the stitching.

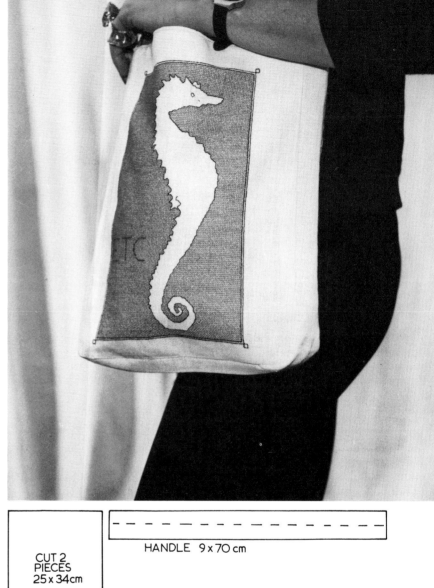

CUT 2
PIECES
25 x 34 cm

HANDLE 9 x 70 cm

GUSSET 5 x 90 cm

FELT 35 x 60 cm

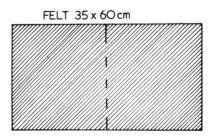

Cut-out instructions for fabric and felt.

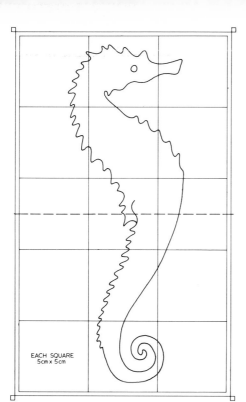

EACH SQUARE
5cm x 5cm

Seahorse shape.

and initials are worked in black back or running stitches. If the drawn initials are not clear through the cross stitches you will have to work 'by eye'.

To make up your bag

Remove the peripheral tape or binding stitches. Machine or hand stitch 1 long side of the gusset panel to the sides and base of the front panel, right sides together. Stitch the other long side of the gusset to the right side of the back panel. Press seams towards the front and back panels, and turn the bag right side out. Turn the top 1.5cm of the bag in and stitch, 3mm below the fold.

To make the handle, fold the remaining long panel lengthwise, right side in, and stitch the sides together to form a tube. Turn this right side out with the tube turner. Pin the handle so that the seam is down the centre of the length and stitch along both long sides, 3mm in from the edges. Place the handle so that 2cm at either end are against the top of the inside of the gusset and stitch with 2 parallel horizontal lines.

Fold the felt in 2 and hold it against the flattened bag. Note the exact width of the bag (including gusset). This will be the width of your lining. Stitch the lining down its side and base.

Place the lining, stitchings out, inside the bag. Turn the top 3mm of lining under and pin it just below the top line of stitching of the bag. Neatly hem the lining to the bag, using 1 strand of orange stranded cotton.

Other ideas for the Assisi seahorse

Why not use this charming little fellow for an Assisi rug? You could work it over a large-mesh canvas. First work the outline of the sea-horse and then fill both his shape *and* the reserves outside with cross stitches.

3 Bargello typewriter cover **

Would that typewriter manufacturers emulated some sewing machine producers and sold their machines in attractive covers: those horrid clear or murky plastic covers bring back memories of typing pools in impersonal offices several decades back.

This is my typewriter cover! The top is worked in 4-way Bargello in 3 shades of purple and lime-green Paternayan persian wool. The skirt is matching purple batiste, and it is attached to the top with velcro so that it can be taken off for machine or hand washing.

You can make a typewriter cover to fit any machine and suit any room. The measurements given below are for a small portable electric Smith–Corona machine.

To make a bargello typewriter cover you will need

> Area of canvas with 30 single threads per 5cm, measurements should be height and width of your typewriter top plus at least 20cm in each direction
> I purchased 225gm hanks of Paternayan persian yarns 615 and 620 medium purples, and 45 strands each of 610 dark purple and G74 lime green
> Area of skirt fabric 24cm high and width enough to go completely round your typewriter (I used John Lewis batiste)
> All-purpose thread to match the skirt fabric
> Blunt needle (I used tapestry 18)
> Velcro 1.5cm wide, length the same as the width of your skirt fabric
> NEPO pen
> Frame if you use one for bargello

Mark out a canvas area the size of your typewriter top and count *holes* to find the centre of your design, NEPO-marking the canvas into eighths. Now you are ready to stitch.

As shown in the chapter on Bargello in *The Coats Book of Embroidery* (p 27ff), Bargello is characterised by parallel rows of different-coloured vertical stitches. For this design the canvas is turned successively through 90°, 180° and 270° to form a 4-way design radiating from the centre. All stitches are *over 6* canvas threads and the step is always *2 threads*. A and B on the basic pattern are pivot stitches. You will be stitching throughout with *2 strands* of thread. As with other fibres strip and put 2 strands back together again for a fluffier effect.

I suggest you start by working a single formation A to B, starting A at a point about 10cm from the centre along your upper vertical marking. When you get to B work a mirror image, back, as it were, to A, and thence to B. Stop when you reach your upper right hand marked diagonal line. Go back to the vertical line and work AB the other side of the line, then BA and so on, stopping when you reach the upper left hand marked diagonal.

Turn the canvas through 90° and count how many threads out from the centre hole your initial stitching was. Count a similar number along what is now your upper vertical line and work another wavy row of stitching to the right diagonal and then a similar row to the left diagonal.

Turn the canvas again through 90°, and again, and repeat the process so that you have a line of stitching continuing around 360°. This is your 'base line' and it sets a key for all subsequent stitching. Having worked this initial line you can now work parallel lines above and below, alternating your colours as required. My particular colour change was lime green—palest purple—medium purple—dark purple—medium purple—palest purple—lime green—palest purple and so on.

If a stitch has to share a hole with an already worked stitch, try always to work with your needle coming up in an empty hole and going down into a partly filled one. Continue working until all your marked 'typewriter shape' is covered. Do not extend beyond that line.

An *attractive* typewriter cover – practical, too, for the skirt can be taken off and machine washed (cover top 29 × 29cm).

After you have marked off a suitable area of canvas, divide it into eighths by counting holes (1). You will work 4-way bargello, which entails turning the canvas through 90°, 180° and 270° (2). Bargello stitches are worked over 6 threads of canvas: steps (b to d in this diagram) are 2 threads deep (3). The complete motif is A to B. Notice that the design pivots on A and B (4).

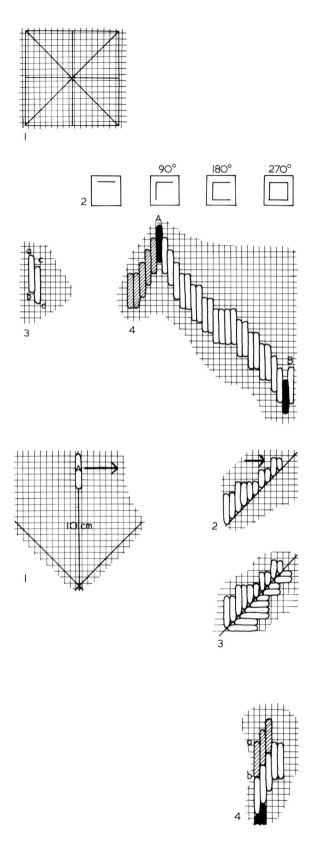

I suggest you begin working the design with A on the upper vertical marking of the canvas. Continue the pattern, towards B and back again and so on, towards the upper right diagonal marking (1). When you reach that marking, continue the pattern as far as you can without crossing the marking (2). You will find that as you turn the canvas around other stitches will work to the other side of the diagonal (3). When you have worked an entire row of stitching all around the canvas work parallel rows, same length stitches in same repeat but with a colour change, above and below. Always try to work from an empty hole to a partly filled one (4).

To make up your cover

You should first form a small hem at each end of your fabric. Make a 3cm (base) hem along 1 of the long sides and turn back and tack, but do not stitch, 1 cm along the long side. Place 1 of the 2 velcro 'sandwich' lengths to cover your 1cm turn back, the edge of the velcro parallel to that of the fabric. Stitch the velcro in place.

I found it easiest to cut my surplus canvas to a width of 2cm. I bound the edges, divided the remaining velcro length in quarters and stitched one quarter to the surplus canvas on each side of the worked area. I trimmed the corner surplus. The skirt can now be fastened to the velcro encompassing the canvas area, and the cover is ready to fit over the machine – the slit formed by both ends of the long skirt piece accommodates the typewriter's cord.

Other ideas relating to this project

Work your initials on your typewriter cover.
Using the above formula, design and work covers for your smaller pieces of kitchen equipment.

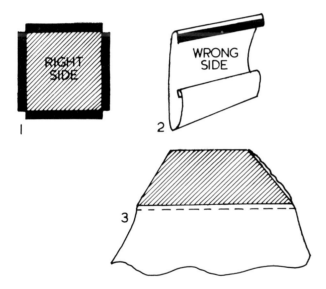

Velcro is sewn to a narrow surplus on the right side of the canvas: corners of the surplus can be carefully trimmed (1). The other velcro strip is sewn to the narrow hem at the top of the skirt strip (2). Velcro can therefore hold the skirt in place (3).

4 Blackwork 'special clutch' ***

I needed a decorative evening bag to go with a plain 'little black dress' and, just at that time, I was looking at some photographs of late 16th-century woodcuts in the Ashmolean Museum, Oxford. Were these woodcuts, perhaps intended as lining papers for little boxes, copied by blackwork embroiderers of the time? Or were the woodcut designs inspired by embroideries? (Which came first, the chicken or the egg?) Certainly the woodcuts have inspired *this* embroiderer of the 20th century!

I designed and made a quilted satin clutch bag with a blackwork motif (see the chapter on blackwork on p 34ff of *The Coats Book of Embroidery*). The same pattern could, alternatively, be made up in an evenweave linen such as Glenshee which would make exact stitch alignment easier. The bag is bound in black to hide possible dirty marks after an evening out.

A late 16th-century woodcut in the Ashmolean Museum.

26

To make my bag you will need

    40cm white satin (I used John Lewis Virginia satin)
    40cm white lining
    40cm vilene belt pelmet sew in, to use as stiffener
    140cm black satin ribbon 1.5cm wide
    1 skein each DMC coton-à-broder and stranded cotton 310
    black
    Black and white all-purpose sewing thread
    8 and 4 crewel needles
    Tracing paper and dressmaker's carbon
    Frame (I used my 15cm round hoop)

The central motif of the woodcut inspired the decoration of this clutch bag, sensibly bound with black satin ribbon.

Cut shapes of satin and lining for the main part of the bag and for 2 gussets. Prepare 1 area of stiffener.

Trace the outline of the main motif and apply it, with carbon paper, to the centre of the main satin and with the bottom of the motif 3cm up from the base of the fabric. Put the marked fabric on the frame.

First work the infilling of the motif. Follow the stitch directions illustrated: I worked 'by eye', as did many of the 16th-century embroiderers, but if you like you can trace the patterns from the illustration on to the relevant parts of the satin. Work patterns 1 to 5 and the 2 upper parts of the main stem in back or double-running stitches, 1 strand of stranded cotton on the crewel 8 needle. Satin stitch is formed with 3 strands of stranded cotton. French knots are worked with 1 thickness of coton-à-broder.

Outline all sections of the motif with coton-à-broder back stitch, 1 thickness.

Cut-out instructions for
fabric, lining and stiffener.

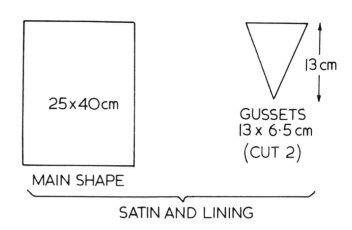

25x40cm

MAIN SHAPE

GUSSETS
13 x 6·5 cm
(CUT 2)

13 cm

SATIN AND LINING

23 x 37·5 cm
STIFFENER

To make up the clutch bag

Remove the satin from the frame and press. Pin it right side up to the stiffening, turn under surplus and tack. With a pencil, mark a trellis on the stiffener, with lines 3cm apart. Working from the stiffener side, sew along all these lines with machine stitching or small running stitches in white all-purpose thread.

Press the lining and fold edges under to produce a shape the same size as the satin and stiffening. Tack the surplus down. Pin the lining to the main shape, wrong sides together, tack and sew all around the edges with neat running stitches close to the edges.

Take a satin and a lining gusset shape and place right sides together. Sew 1cm in from edges, leaving 4cm along one of the longer sides unstitched. Carefully remove surplus fabric at corners and turn the shape right side out. Oversew the open edge. Tack around the shape and press. Do the same with the other gusset pieces.

Starting with a corner at the far end of the motif, oversew the main shape to one of the gusset long sides, from the broad end towards the point. When you reach that point, carefully fold the main shape over and carry on oversewing along the other long side of the gusset. Do the same with the other side of the main shape, attaching it to the other gusset.

Now carefully hem black satin ribbon over all edges and you have a neatly bound white clutch bag. Have a happy evening!

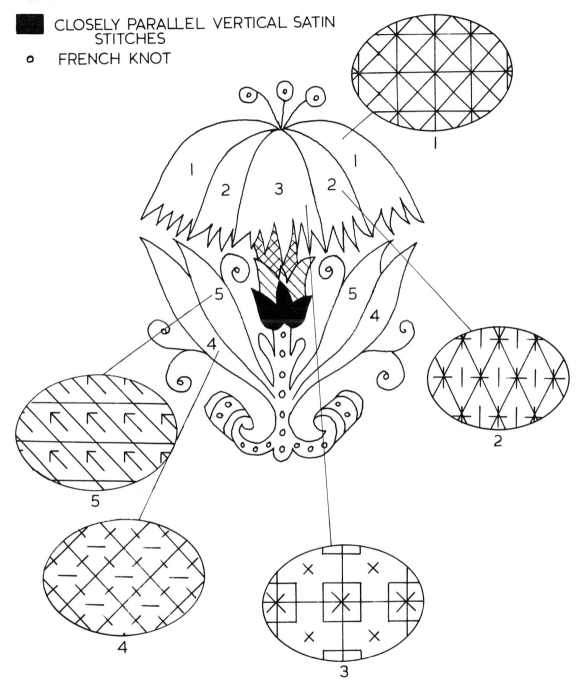

CLOSELY PARALLEL VERTICAL SATIN
STITCHES

○ FRENCH KNOT

Blackwork motif.

5 Broderie anglaise housecoat **

A friend was shopping in Palm Beach recently for an attractive lightweight housecoat. I could not believe the price of what was available. A hundred dollars (at that time nearly £50) for *that?* I made some mental notes – and came home and designed my own.

My housecoat is mid-calf length with elbow-length sleeves. It has frills around the neck, front opening, hem and sleeves. I made it in a pale blue easy-care batiste and I worked a broderie anglaise design on each upper front panel in a matching stranded cotton.

I can wear it as a dressing gown. It packs beautifully and, worn with a gold belt and gold sandals, it makes an attractive dinner gown.

To make a broderie anglaise housecoat you will need

3m of lightweight fabric (I used a Jonelle batiste, pale blue, 117cm wide)
2 cards (3m each) of matching bias binding
All-purpose sewing thread to match
2 skeins DMC stranded cotton (I used 598 blue)
Pointed needle (I used 8 crewel)
Paper to make your own pattern
Tracing paper and carbon for transferring the broderie anglaise motif
Frame (I used my 15cm round hoop)

Following the paper pattern-making instructions, make paper shapes from the illustration here. Now cut out, in fabric, 2 front garment panels, 1 back panel, 2 sleeve frills and 4 other frill lengths for the neck, front openings and main hem.

You will probably find it easier to make the garment and then site the embroidery exactly. Stitch the fronts to the back panel, joining shoulder and upper sleeve seams and under sleeve and side seams.

Join a sleeve frill to make a tube as illustrated. Fit the gathered frill to the *right* (outer) side of 1 of the sleeves. Stitch, trim the surplus and cover the seam with bias binding. Form the other sleeve frill in the same way. To make the main frill, join all 4 remaining frill panels to form a long circle. Fold it according to the illustration, gather, fit it to the *right* side of the housecoat, stitch, trim the surplus and cover the seam with bias binding.

You are now ready to embroider. Decide exactly where on one of the front panels you would like the motif sited and, using tracing paper and carbon, draw out the design. Working from the reverse of your carbon drawing, make a mirror image on the other front panel.

All the 'circles and hoops' of your design are worked in a similar manner in *3 strands* of stranded cotton. Think of each shape as a circular (or oval) wheel. First put on 'inner tyres' by working little running stitches just around the outside of each marking.

Now an area of the design should be put on your frame or hoop.

This batiste housecoat is easy to make – and is ultra feminine with frills and broderie anglaise embroidery.

Cut-out instructions for the housecoat. Cut 2 similar shapes for the back and front. Then cut the front panel in 2, down the fold line, and remove areas shaded on the diagram. Two sleeve frills can be cut from surplus under the arms. The remaining fabric should be cut into 4 to give frill strips 17.5cm high.

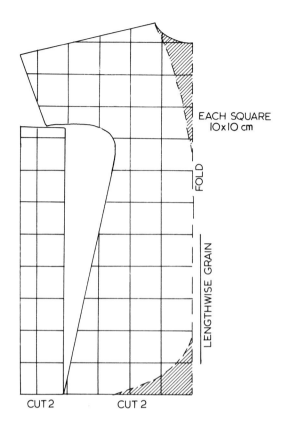

To form a sleeve frill, the strip is folded vertically and a tube sewn. This tube is then folded horizontally and the 2 edges are gathered.

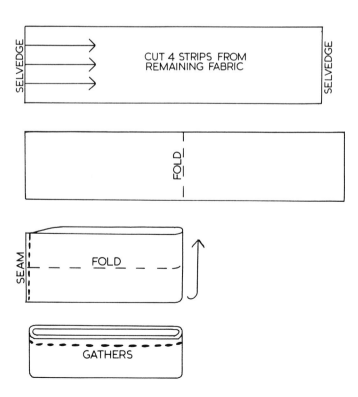

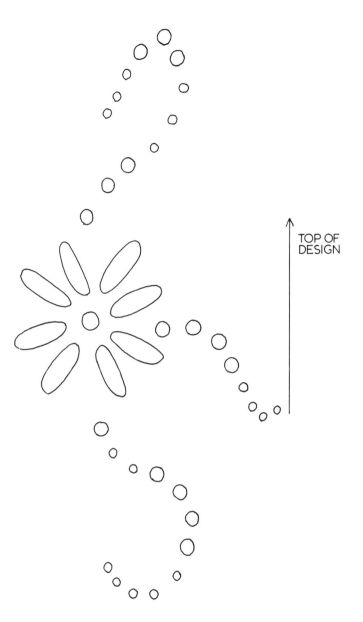

Broderie anglaise motif. It can be sited wherever you like when you have made the garment.

TOP OF DESIGN

Remove the inside of all the wheels in the manner illustrated – traditionally all broderie anglaise holes were cut with a pointed stiletto but you can use sharp-pointed embroidery scissors. When a hole has been cut to provide the main 'tyre', work around with neat binding satin stitches from the outside of the wheel in to the hole. All your stitches should aim towards the hub of the 'wheel'.

Remember that you want the reverse of the work – the inside of your housecoat – to be as neat as possible. Start a new embroidery thread by working 1 or 2 minute back stitches in an area that will be covered by subsequent binding stitchings. Finish a thread in a similar manner or weave it neatly in and out on the reverse of a worked area.

If you like you can produce fatter 'tyres' by padding some of the areas subsequently to be covered by binding satin stitches.

Your housecoat is now finished. Doesn't it look worth a hundred dollars at least?

Broderie anglaise.
Traditionally a stiletto
(shaded here) was used to
cut holes but a sharp pair of
scissors can be used instead.

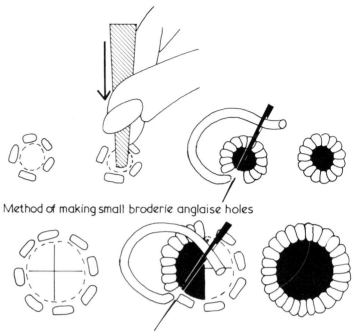

Method of making small broderie anglaise holes

Larger holes are formed by cutting fabric and
turning segments back

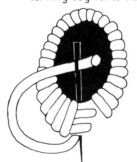

PADDED BRODERIE ANGLAISE

Other ideas relating to this design

From the surplus fabric (under the arms of the back or front panels) form pockets or a bandeau.

Draw freehand, with a light pencil or invisible pen marker, leaves and stems around the cut-out holes. Work the former in closely parallel satin stitches and the latter in neat stem stitches.

Use the same instructions to make a shorter or longer garment:

To make a short bedjacket, you will need only 2m of fabric. Shorten the paper pattern 50cm from underarm to hem. Join the 2 shortened sleeve frill lengths to form 1 frill and make the other sleeve's frill from 1 of the 4 main frill lengths. Use only 3 frill lengths to fit the neck, front opening and main hem edges.

To make a full-length housecoat, you should purchase 4m of fabric. Lengthen the paper pattern 30cm from underarm to hem. Do not lengthen the sleeve frills. Cut 6 main frills 17.5cm wide to fit the edges of the neck, front openings and main hem of your housecoat – but before you fit these frills try the garment on as it must be shortened, if necessary, before the frills are added.

6 Cards for all occasions *

Many people are scared at the thought of stitching on paper. It tears. Every wrong needle-prick shows.

In the past many exquisitely delicate pictures were formed on fine papers (see the illustration on p 50 of *The Coats Book of Embroidery*). I first experimented with working on brown wrapping paper backed with self-adhesive vinyl. When I had mastered this I progressed to stitching on postcard-type card.

Children, too, love stitching on card. Cards for all occasions can be fun and simple to work, and the materials are not expensive.

You can make birthday, Christmas and Valentine cards. You can make signs to hang on your bedroom door.

If you master and develop this basic 'card recipe' you will find that you can design and stitch cards for a myriad of purposes.

For the basic card recipe you will need (for each card)

> 1 postcard (I used an 8.7 × 14cm size)
> Selection of threads (see below)
> Pointed needle (I used crewel 4)
> Soft-lead pencil and eraser

Fun and simple-to-make stitched cards for a variety of occasions and places.

The basic instructions for all my cards are the same. First you lightly draw your design on the right side of the card. Then knot a length of thread on your needle (when stitching with this recipe you cannot worry about how the reverse of your work will look and you start each new thread with a knot). Stitch over all your pencil markings, remembering:

1 you cannot rectify a mistake as a wrong needle-prick will show;
2 you should not take too small stitches or the paper between holes will tear;
3 if you are working a solid block it is a good idea to stitch just on the outside rather than the inside of the pencil marking as then the pencil will be covered by stitching;
4 if you are line-stitching around a circle, stitch slightly on the outside rather than the inside of the pencil marking.

Finish each thread by weaving in and out, on the reverse, of worked stitches.

When you have finished all your stitching, carefully erase any pencil marks that show.

Variations on the basic card recipe include:

Christmas card

As well as the basic card recipe materials you will need:

> 1 skein DMC coton-à-broder 895 dark green
> Small amount DMC gold embroidery thread
> Area of stiffened paper or light card at least twice as large as your basic card (I used yellow lightweight card 20 × 15cm)
> An appropriate envelope to fit the above paper or card folded in half
> Tracing paper and carbon
> Copydex adhesive

Trace the Christmas tree and stars outline on to your basic card. Stitch the tree in green back stitches (my stitches were about 3mm long). Form the stars with big crosses of gold thread. Erase any tracing marks.

Fold the stiffened paper or card in half and fix the card, wrong side down, to the centre of the front with adhesive. Write your message inside – and your card is all ready to go!

Thank you card

What is nicer than a home-made 'thank you' card after a party, a weekend or whatever? As well as the basic card recipe you will need:

> 1 skein each DMC coton-à-broder 351 geranium and 814 dark red
> Another area of card the same size as your basic card
> Adhesive

In your ordinary handwriting, write your message on the right side of your basic card. Now stitch that message in back stitches about 3mm long: I wrote: 'Thank you' in dark red and the rest in geranium. Erase any pencil marks.

Fix the wrong side of the stitched card to the wrong side of the

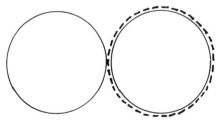

When stitching to a pencilled circle (dotted here), always stitch outside rather than inside the pencil marks.

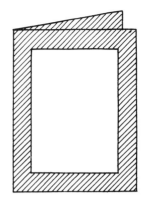

Christmas card design. When finished, the stitched card is fixed to the front of a folded paper or card (shaded here).

ACTUAL SIZE

other card with adhesive. Now you can write the name and address of the recipient on the right side of that other card, stick on a stamp and your 'thank you' is all ready to send!

Smile sign

To meet my moody blues and Monday morning horrors I made this sign for my bedroom door. As well as the basic card recipe you will need, to make a similar sign:

    1 skein each DMC coton-à-broder 321 red and 797 blue
    Hole punch
    Ruler
    Tracing paper and carbon

Trace the design on to the front of your card and stitch it in back stitches about 3mm long. All is worked in red except for the face and its features, which are worked in blue. Erase any pencil marks.

Carefully find the half-way point along the top of your card and punch a hole there. Make a loop of red thread about 10cm long, when doubled, and your card can be hung on your door or above your bed to cheer you up each morning!

Other ideas from the basic card recipe

Use a larger sheet of card to write out a favourite poem or the Lord's Prayer to hang in your room.

Use a long and narrow sheet of card to write out the alphabet for a toddler's room.

From a very long and narrow sheet of card you could make a wall-measure to see how tall you and others are. Carefully measure exact centimetres and stitch marks. Hang the finished stitched measure at the appropriate height.

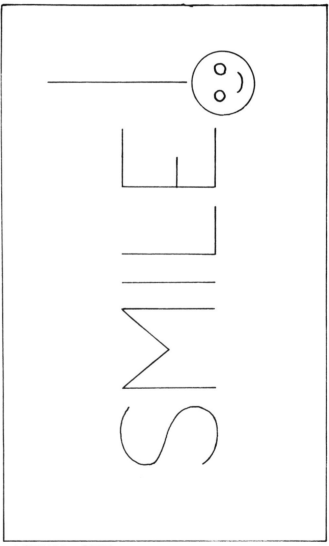

Hanging notice pattern.

ACTUAL SIZE

7 Chainstitched games boards *

Children on the beach . . . family groups on picnics . . . anyone travelling, who not only wants to take his board games with him but would appreciate having a soft fabric cloth to add padding when packing his luggage . . . these games boards are designed for just such occasions!

I made my portable chess and backgammon boards from large squares of brightly-coloured felt. They are marked with applied felt bits and embellished with chainstitch. My chess board is lime green with black squares and golden stitching and the stitched area measures 34 × 34cm: the backgammon board is orange with dark green felt appliqué and black stitching and the stitched area measures 39 × 39cm.

You will find both these boards easy and fun to make. The only embroidery technique required is chainstitch.

To make a chess board you will need

> Felt for the main board 60 × 60cm (I used lime green)
> A second colour of felt 30 × 30cm (I used black)
> DMC pearl cotton 5 (I used 973 golden)
> All-purpose thread in the colour of your second felt
> Pointed needles (I used crewel 2 and 9)
> Graph paper

First cut out a paper template 4 × 4cm from your graph paper, and use this template to cut out 32 squares of black felt each 4 × 4cm.

Lay these squares on the main felt in 'chess board' style, the tips of the black squares touching but not overlapping. Pin the squares in place and sew them, with all-purpose thread on a fine needle, to the main felt, with tiny running stitches close to the edges of the black felts.

Now you cover these little running stitches with pearl cotton chainstitch on a thicker needle. Work chainstitches in straight lines from one side to the other of the whole area of the application, as in the diagram. Chainstitch around the perimeter of this area, and then work another peripheral row of stitching 1cm outside, working corner 'tassels' as shown.

To make a backgammon board you will need

> Felt for the main board 60 × 60cm (I used bright orange)
> A second colour of felt 40 × 20cm (I used dark green)
> DMC pearl cotton 5 (I used 310 black)
> All-purpose thread in the colour of your second felt
> Pointed needles (I used crewel 2 and 9)
> Graph paper

Cut a graph-paper triangular template as illustrated, and use this to make 24 felt triangles from your second felt.

A chess board made of felt so
that it can be taken with
you wherever you go.

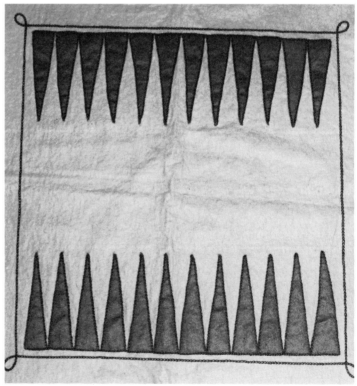

The backgammon board is
also made of felt.

Lay 12 of these triangles, touching each other but not over-lapping, their bases (the shortest edges) on an imaginary line 12cm from one edge of the main felt. Pin them in place and sew them to the main felt, with tiny running stitches (all-purpose thread on the finer needle) close to the edge of each felt triangle.

Lay the other 12 triangles in a corresponding line, the points of these triangles 14cm from those of the first line (make sure that this second line is exactly in alignment, facing down to the first line). Similarly pin and stitch.

Now you chainstitch all around each triangle (pearl cotton on the thicker needle). When you reach a point you should stop your line of stitching and start another one, as in the diagram.

Measure 1cm outside the whole area of application and work a peripheral line of chainstitch, with corner tassels as shown.

And now you are ready to play! All you need is a partner – and men, pieces and dice as required.

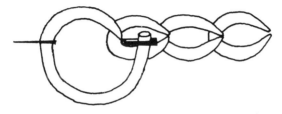

Chainstitch

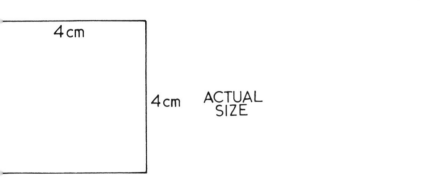

4 cm

4 cm   ACTUAL
SIZE

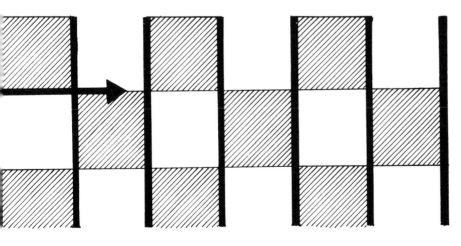

You need to make 32 squares, 4 × 4cm, from your second felt. When the squares are placed in position on the main felt, they are first neatly held with running stitches and then chainstitch (here black) is worked from one side of the whole decorated area to the other.

41

24 triangular pieces should be cut from your second felt. When they are stitched in place, with little running stitches, chainstitch is worked around the edges. When you reach a point, finish that line of stitching (1) and begin another line (2).

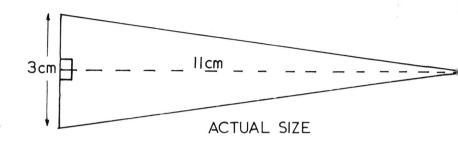

ACTUAL SIZE

3cm   11cm

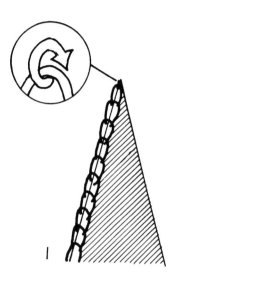

Other ideas for this travelling game formula

Personalise a chess board by putting initials or relevant dates on each applied square of felt, and give the finished board to granny or grandad for Christmas.

Design your own chainstitch-on-felt maze, a perennial source of fascination and challenge.

Make your own little chess pieces. You can use the box formula (next) to form the pieces, which can be identified by embroidered motifs of a bishop's mitre, horse's head, king's crown and so on.

8 Couch a little box**

Little boxes, little boxes . . . many people collect boxes of all kinds
and others long to have more. Some boxes are useful. Others are
purely decorative.

  This little box is fun to make and I shall use it as a jewellery
container. It measures 5 × 10 × 6cm, and the outside is purple felt,
the inside bright pink felt. The top is decorated with a couched
pre-Columbian motif. Around the sides are couched lines in battlement formation. The lid can be opened with the co-ordinating tassel.

To make my couched box you will need

> 2 squares of different colours of felt each 20cm square (I used
> purple and bright pink)
> A similar amount of sturdy canvas (I used 14 mono with
> plenty of sizing); this will provide the stiffener
> 3 skeins DMC stranded cotton, one to match the felt for the
> outside of the box and the others complementary (I used
> 1 skein each 550 deep purple, 553 paler purple, 807 duck egg blue)
> All-purpose sewing thread to match the outside felt
> Pointed needles (I used 9 and 4 crewel)
> Tracing paper and carbon
> Frame (I used a 15 × 15cm artist's stretcher)

Felt box (all stitching and no
glue!) decorated with a
typical pre-Columbian motif.
All the embellishment is
couched.

Cut-out instructions for both pieces of felt: when cutting canvas stiffener shapes make them 1mm smaller in each direction.

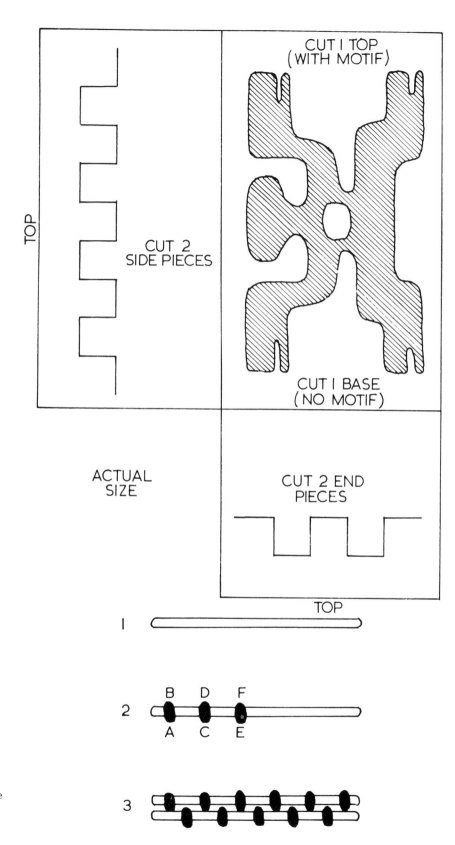

CUT I TOP
(WITH MOTIF)

TOP

CUT 2
SIDE PIECES

CUT I BASE
(NO MOTIF)

ACTUAL
SIZE

CUT 2 END
PIECES

TOP

Couching: the laying thread (white) is laid from 1 side to the other of the area to be covered. It is then held with small couchings in another thread (black here). Couchings should be perpendicular to the laid thread and about 4mm from each other. Subsequent rows are similarly worked, with couchings in brick formation (in this diagram there is intentionally a small gap between rows, although in fact you should stitch as close to the previous line as you can).

Use your tracing paper and carbon to draw outlines and embroidery sitings on box shapes on your outer and inner felts but do not cut out the shapes as it is easier to embroider on a large area of felt.

Fit the appropriate area of felt on your frame and prepare to embroider the shaded part of the pre-Columbian motif. Thread *6* strands – stripped and put back together – of one of your subsidiary colours (I used the paler purple) on your larger needle. This will be your *laying* thread. Thread *1* strand of the other subsidiary colour (my duck egg blue) on the finer needle. This will be your *couching* thread.

You can read all about complicated couching forms in *The Coats Book of Embroidery* (p 67ff). I worked my motif, however, in a simple brick formation.

First 'lay' your laying thread horizontally across any area of the motif (it is easiest to begin with a line that can go straight across, say from one upper knee to the other). Follow the illustration to see how you should then 'couch' this thread with neat couching stitches, at right angles to the laid thread and about 4mm from each other. When you have finished couching this first line, take a minute back stitch, on the marked outline, with the laying thread and bring it back again to the other side of the area, closely parallel to the first laid thread. Similarly couch this thread, with couching stitches 4mm apart but in *brick* formation to the couchings of the first line (these second row couchings only couch the second laid thread).

Fill the whole of the shaded area of the drawn motif with rows of couching worked in this manner.

Now outline the whole motif, and the hole, with as laying thread 6 strands of your main colour (my darker purple) and the couching thread 1 strand of that same colour (also my darker purple). This outline couching should cover the little back stitches and any other messiness at the edges of the interior couchings.

If necessary adjust the frame and prepare to embroider the sides and ends of the box. All the battlements are worked in 3 closely parallel lines of couching. All laying threads are 6 strands and are couched with 1 strand of the same colour. I worked a line of my main (darker purple) thread at the top, beneath it a line of a subsidiary thread (pale blue) and at the bottom of the trio of lines the other subsidiary thread (paler purple). Make sure that you use the same formation for all the sides and end panels.

Now you can carefully cut out felt shapes for the outside and inside of the box. Also cut out canvas shapes, making them 1mm smaller in each direction than their felt counterparts.

Make a sandwich for each facet of the box, with a canvas held between one colour felt and another colour felt shape. Since you are working with canvas stiffener (rather than, say, unwieldy card) you can pin through all 3 layers. Tack around, and then neatly join the 2 felts together with buttonhole stitches (all purpose sewing thread on your finer needle). Prepare all 6 sandwiched shapes in this manner.

To form the box, lay 2 adjacent shapes together, inside felts together. Oversew their common edge, your stitches threading in and out of the buttonholings. In this manner join the box base to sides and ends. Join sides and ends together, but only join 1 of the longer side panels to the upper (head) edge of the box's top panel.

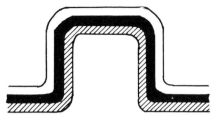

To form the battlement decoration, lay and couch one thread (white here). Parallel to it another thread (black here) is similarly laid and couched, and another (shaded here). Couchings are not shown on this diagram.

You can make a tassel for
the lid of the box by winding
threads around 2 suitable
posts, say 2 fingers. Another
thread (black) is passed
through the loop, which is
removed from the posts and
tied with binding. The (black)
thread ends are attached to
the buttonhole edging of the
box lid (shaded) and the loop
ends cut and trimmed as
required.

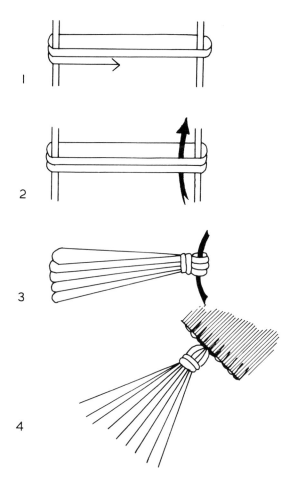

To make a tassel for the lid of your box

Wrap lengths of 6 strands of all your 3 colours around 2 suitable
fixtures (I wrapped, with my right hand, around the thumb and little
finger of my left hand as they were extended). You will need at least
20 wrappings in all. Thread a length of your main thread through
this loop. Remove the loop and bind it tightly, with a main thread,
as close as possible to where the thread goes through it. Secure this
binding thread with 1 or 2 small back stitches. Secure the 2 ends of
the unattached thread with little back stitches worked in and out of
the buttonhole stitch edging in the middle of the lower, feet, side of
the box lid. Cut the loop end and trim to the required length.

Other ideas relating to this box project

You could work with metal threads instead of stranded cottons. In
this case you cannot take the metal laying thread through the
surface of the felt. You must 'plunge' or 'sink' both ends, either
with a heavy 'sinking needle' or by making a loop with another
thread.
Instead of working on felt you may prefer a sumptuous brocade or
similar rich material. Before you cut out your shapes you should
apply an iron-on interfacing such as Vilene Soft Iron-On to prevent
the edges of the shapes subsequently fraying or unravelling.

9 Crewel mirror surround **

In the past, especially in England in the 17th century, women often embroidered pretty surrounds for their mirrors. Narcissistically, perhaps, they enjoyed looking at their faces framed in beauty.

Actually it *is* lovely to have an attractive mirror frame, and this is why I have designed this crewel surround in soft pink, blue, green, mustard and brown wools on best-quality Belgian linen. I hope you will enjoy working it.

To make the crewel mirror surround you will need

> 30cm Elsa Williams Belgian linen (132cm wide, you need only a 30 × 30cm area), 40202 Natural
> 1 card each Elsa Williams crewel wool, 5–4 blue, 13–3 mustard, 9–5 pale pink, 9–3 darker pink, 13–2 lighter brown, 24–1 dark brown and 4–4 green
> Pointed needle (say crewel 4)
> Mirror tile about 10.8cm square
> Area of strong white card 20cm square, corners rounded, with central square cut out, 8.6 × 8.6cm, corners rounded
> Copydex adhesive
> Tracing paper and dressmaker's carbon
> Frame (say 20cm hoop)

First transfer, with tracing paper and carbon, the outline design, repeating the pattern printed here 4 times on the linen. Place an appropriate area of the fabric on the frame.

Since too-long lengths of crewel wool sometimes 'fuzz' it is a good idea to stitch with not more than about 35cm of thread at a time.

An embroidered mirror frame would make a lovely gift: this surround is worked with a crewel design (total size of surround 20 × 20cm).

47

Cut-out instructions for crewel mirror surround: repeat this pattern four times to produce the whole design.

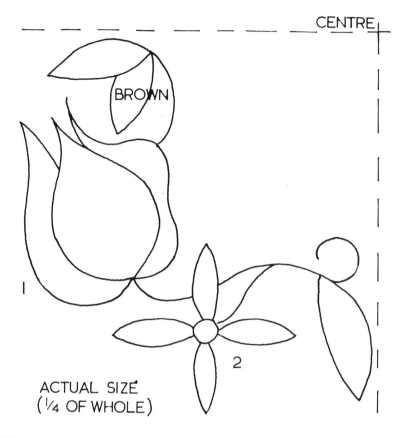

ACTUAL SIZE
(¼ OF WHOLE)

Flowers no 1

The diagram explains the techniques employed here. First work long pale pink straight stitches from one side to the other of the central area to form a trellis, with spaces about 3mm wide. Then darker pink cross stitches are worked over the intersections of the trellis. Outline the tip of the central part of the flower with pale pink stem stitch. Outline the inner sides of the outsides of the flower with pale mustard chainstitch worked from the stem out. Shade the rest of the outsides of the flower with similar rows of chainstitch, with paler brown rows on the insides and darker brown on the outsides of the areas.

Flowers no 2

The petals are infilled with blue fly stitch worked from the outside of the shapes in, and the areas are then outlined with blue chainstitch similarly worked from the outside tip. The centre of the flower is filled with pale mustard french knots.

Leaves

These are all worked, from the stem out, with leaf stitch. Check the diagram to see which leaves are green and which are beige.

Stems

Dark brown stem stitch.

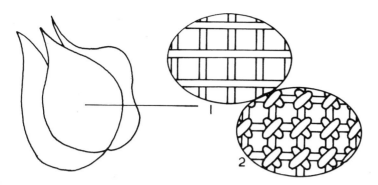

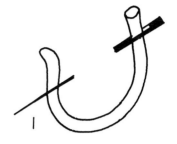

The big flowers (number 1 on the pattern) are infilled with long straight stitches (1) subsequently held with cross stitches (2). Segments either side of this area are worked in lines of cross stitch emanating from the outer tips of the flower.

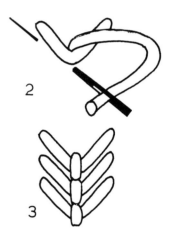

When you have finished your embroidery, take the linen off the frame. Place the fabric right side up over the card shape and note where the large flowers (flowers no 1) lie. Remove the fabric and put the smallest amount of copydex on the card in these spots. Replace the fabric on the card and make sure the fabric lies smooth. Turn the surround over and, from the card side, make 2 diagonal cuts in the central linen, almost – but not quite – to the corners of the visible area.

Working with each flap in turn, spread copydex on an appropriate area of the card and fold a flap of fabric over and on to the card.

Trim the outer surplus of fabric to 5cm around the outside of the card. Make slits around the corners as in the diagram, almost – but not quite – to the card.

Spread copydex on an appropriate corner and fold the corner flap over and on to the card. Hold this in place by placing more copydex and similarly sealing its neighbours. Hold this in place by similarly sealing their neighbours and so on. When all the corners are thus held seal the main side flaps in the same way.

Press the surround for several days in a sandwich of tissue paper under several heavy books.

To attach the surround to the mirror tile, place the smallest amount of copydex to the periphery of the mirror side of the tile. Place the surround, card side down, on to the copydex and press the

Fly stitch.

Stem stitch.

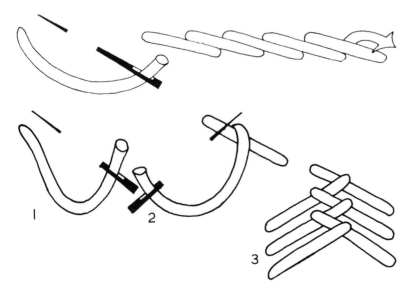

Leaf stitch.

To make up the mirror frame, lay the card (here shaded) on the wrong side of the fabric. Interior diagonal cuts form flaps folded back over the card (1). Outer surplus is trimmed to width of 5cm and cuts made at corners. Segments arrowed are turned back first (2). See the text for adhesive instruction.

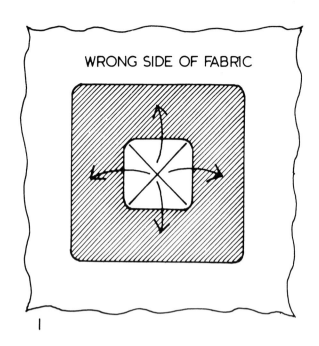

WRONG SIDE OF FABRIC

I

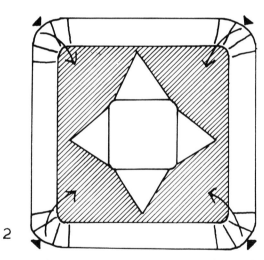

2

partnership under tissue paper with weights only over the mirrored area (you do not want to weight the outer areas of the surround).

Your tile should have self-adhesive pads already attached to it – so you can now 'hang' your mirror wherever you want!

Other ideas for making a similar mirror surround

Work with a larger mirror tile and adjust the sizing of the crewel surround accordingly.

Using the above formula you could work a blackwork surround: adapt the outline design so that it is completely worked with black threads.

Alternatively, follow the design completely in DMC gold embroidery thread to produce a golden wedding present.

10 Cross stitch sampler trio **

From my basic sampler 'recipe' you can design and work your own personalised piece for any occasion. Here I have shown birth, marriage and stately home samplers, but using my formula you can make, for instance, a special Christmas sampler. You can work as many, or as few, motifs on your sampler as you like.

For a basic sampler 28 × 15.5cm you will need

Aida fabric with 27 blocks per 5cm, piece 40 × 25cm
Anchor stranded cottons as required
Talon or DMC metallic silver thread as required
24 tapestry needle
Sheet and scraps of graph paper
Pencils

How to plan your sampler

First design your sampler on your sheet of graph paper. Mark the vertical half-way line: this will be the centre of your piece. Note that 1 square of graph paper = 1 block of fabric and each stitch will be worked over one of those fabric blocks.

Copy my basic sampler drawing on your graph sheet. You now have the rest of the space within the outer border to fill as you want. Remember to make your design symmetrical and to 'centre' any inscriptions.

To centre your inscriptions

First, following the lettering at the top of the basic sampler drawing, jot down your inscription on a scrap of graph paper. Make sure you do not fill more than 76 squares across (there are 76 available blocks of fabric inside the outer border of your sampler). Count to find the vertical centre of your written inscription (if you have filled an odd number of squares, one 'side' will occupy one more square than the other). Now, using the central marking on your scrap paper, draw the inscription, centred, on to your main paper sampler pattern.

When you have finished your drawing, you can start stitching on the aida fabric.

Stitches (Stitch diagrams are given at the back of the book)

Back stitch: 1 or 3 strands as stated
Cross stitch: 1 strand for all lettering, otherwise 3 strands

To make a birth sampler

I made a cheerful bright-red sampler for my niece Leila Rached. First the basic sampler recipe was drawn on the graph paper, and then I added the motifs illustrated here.

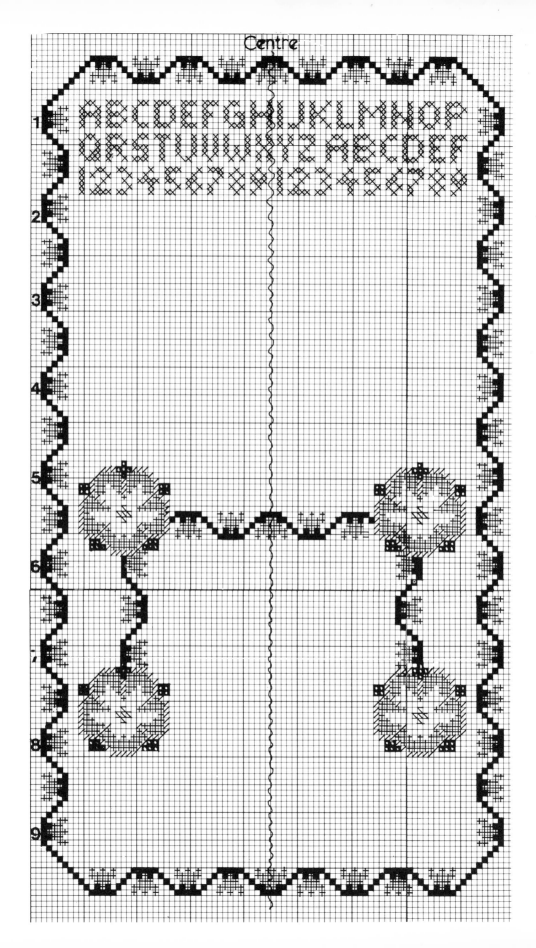

A finished birth sampler worked on bright red aida cloth.

Diagram for the birth sampler. The angel, ship, butterfly and small flower should be reversed on the other side.

Stitching details

On red aida cloth,

Cross stitch:

■ ◘ 0255 parrot green – all 3 strands
⊬ 0290 canary yellow – all 3 strands
× 0402 white – 1 strand
+ 0402 white – 3 strands
/ 0160 kingfisher – 3 strands

Back stitch:

— 0290 canary yellow or 0160 kingfisher

To make a marriage sampler

Rick and Annies' wedding required, I felt, a really personal present I had made myself. This sampler incorporates traditional wedding bells, Chinese longevity signs, hearts and lovebirds. As before, first I drew on graph paper my basic sampler recipe and then I added marriage motifs.

Stitching details

On pale blue aida cloth,

Cross stitch:

■ ◘ 0267 moss green – 3 strands
+ 0161 kingfisher – 3 strands
○ 0402 white – 3 strands
× 0401 grey – 1 strand
/ 1 reel Talon silver – double thickness

To make a 'stately home' sampler

You may like to work your own home as a sampler (but I personally thought that our little brick house in Dorset was not as sampler-genic as a stately home in Lincolnshire we had recently visited!).

First I drew out the basic sampler recipe and added the other 'home' motifs illustrated. Then I drew a facade view of Doddington and inserted that. (If you prefer your own or another house, draw it first on a scrap of graph paper, centre the design and insert it in the appropriate place.)

Stitching details

On pale green aida cloth

Cross stitch:

■ 0261 almond green – 3 strands
+ 010 geranium – 3 strands
○ 06 geranium – 3 strands
/ 0351 chestnut – 3 strands
◘ 0269 moss green – 3 strands
× 0360 peat brown – 1 strand
∅ 0169 peacock blue – 3 strands
\ 0292 buttercup – 3 strands

Back stitch:

— 0360 peat brown – 1 strand (house details) – but otherwise 0269 moss green (3 strands), for leaves, acorns etc

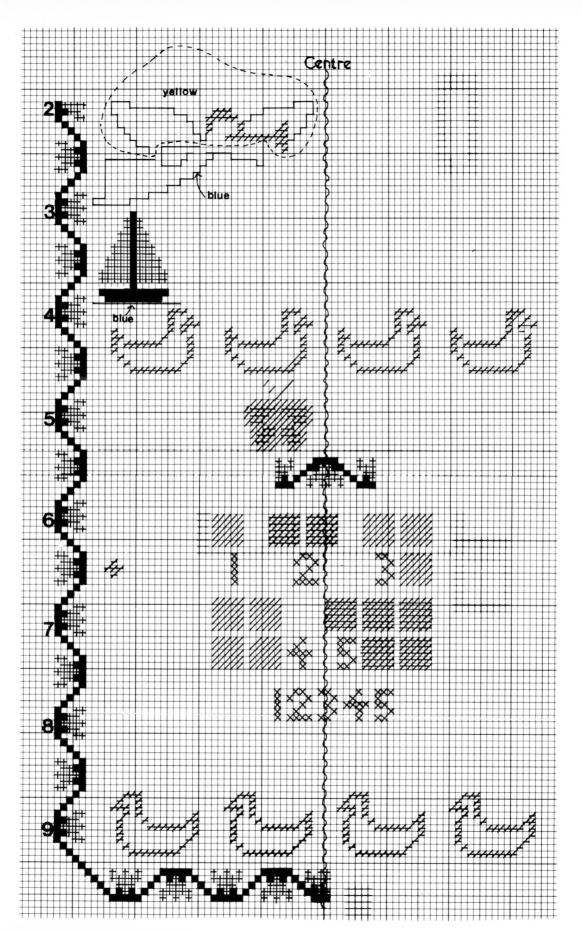

yellow

blue

Centre

blue

2

3

4

5

6

7

8

9

opposite Diagram of wedding sampler details: continue the lines of hearts and horseshoes across and work similar flowers, the other half of the longevity sign and a mirror-image lovebird in the other half.

Wedding sampler on pale blue aida.

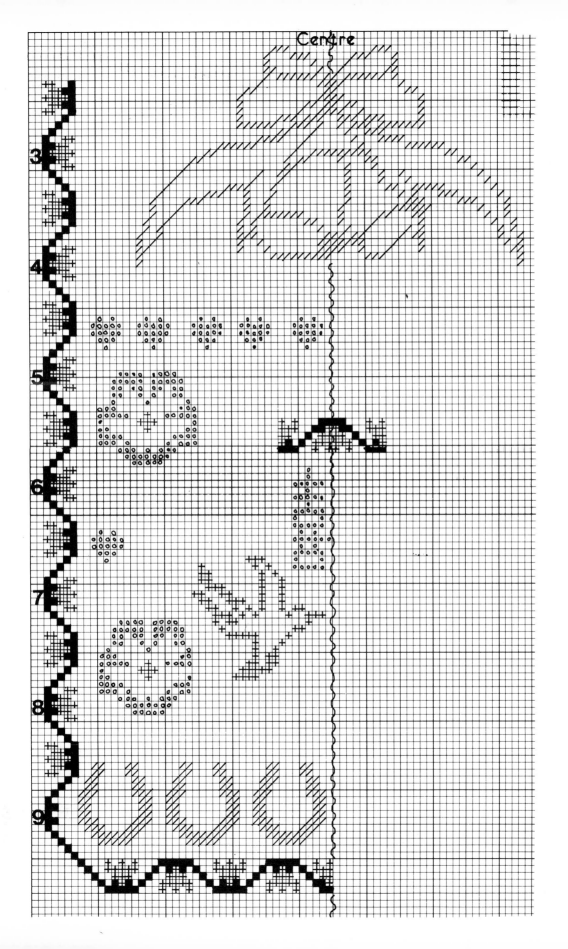

Centre

opposite Add these details to the basic recipe to produce your 'home' sampler.

Stately home sampler (although you may prefer to work the front of your own house).

The pattern for the front of Doddington Hall, Lincolnshire.

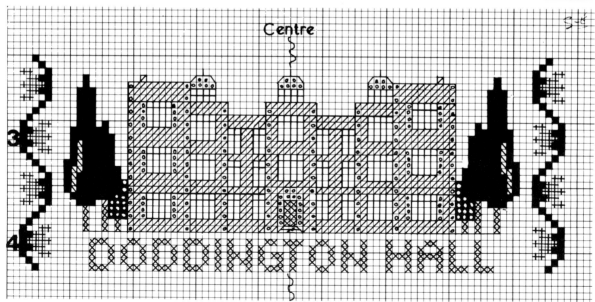

11 Pattern darn a skirt *

A useful dirndl skirt
embellished with different
coloured pattern darning
co-ordinates with several tops.

I realised I had lots of tops but nothing suitable to wear with them, so . . . I made a skirt. It complements no less than three different tops and now I have three fashionable outfits.

The skirt is in dirndl style, gathered into an easy-to-make waistband. I used a pale pink linen-type fabric and embellished the skirt in two shades of green and one of blue.

To make the pattern darned skirt you will need

> 90cm linen or linen-type fabric with recognisable evenweave (150cm wide)
> 3 skeins (or more) of DMC coton-à-broder (I used 906 light green, 895 dark green and 798 blue)
> Tapestry needle 20
> All-purpose sewing thread to match your fabric
> 18cm zip fastener to match the fabric
> Soft pencil
> Ruler
> Frame (I used my 20cm hoop)

This is a garment that you make first and then embellish. First, cut your fabric as indicated. Place the 2 skirt pieces together, right sides in, and completely stitch 1 side seam from top to bottom of the skirt. Leave the top 20cm of the other seam unstitched, ready for the zip.

Everyone has her favourite method of putting in a zip. My 'quickie' for such a garment is to turn back both sides of the fabric and sew close to the folds. I then pin, tack and sew 1 of the sides to 1 side of the zip. Then I tack the other side of the fabric just overlapping the other, stitched, side, and I machine this second side in place.

After you have put in the zip, gather around the top of the skirt. Put the waist strip around your waist and (honestly!) mark how long your waistband should be. Divide this length in half. Pull the gathers of the skirt so that one of the skirt panels fits one-half of your waist 'measurement' and the other fits the other half, and stitch the skirt to the band accordingly, right sides together. Fold the

Cut-out for pattern darned
skirt.

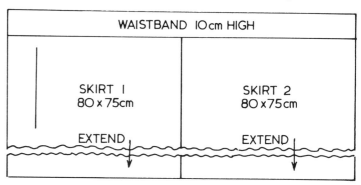

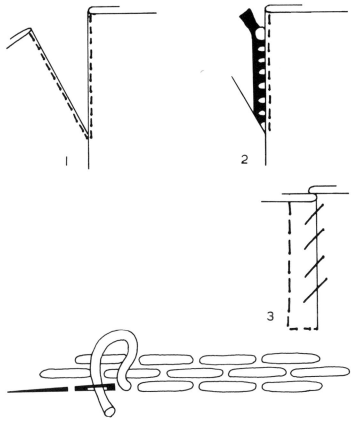

One quick method of putting in a zip fastener: turn back both sides of fabric to continue the 'seam line' below, and machine stitch close to the folds (1). Place the zip behind one of the stitched folds and stitch close to the teeth of the zip (2). Place the other stitched fold just in front of the one holding the zip and tack it in place. Machine this other panel to the zip (3).

Darning consists of parallel lines of long running stitches forming a required pattern.

waistband over and neatly hem it to the inside of the garment, and turn under both ends of the waistband. Attach hooks and eyes as required.

Now try the skirt on and turn up the hem to the required length. Press – and you are ready to embellish.

You have a skirt with easily recognisable weft threads parallel to the hem of your garment. You are going to make up your own pattern darning design and stitch it in your own choice of colours.

As its name implies this technique consists of darning, long running stitches, worked in a pattern. I decided to work a simple formation of stitches 1.5cm long and to get the first row of stitching right I measured and made tiny pencil dots 1.5cm apart on the same weft thread all around the skirt, 10cm up from the hem.

Then I put an area of the skirt on my hoop and made my first row of stitches, taking up 2 threads of the fabric at each pencil dot. I worked all around the skirt, moving the hoop as necessary. When I had completed a 'circle' I worked another circuit, 2 weft threads up from the first, with each stitch 2 warp threads over from its predecessor. I worked a third dark green row in similar spiral alignment. Continuing in this manner I then worked 2 blue rows and 1 lighter green. I did a similar band 3cm above the first band.

So simple – such fun to work and so effective! I did not do much decoration on my skirt: you might like to do rows and rows of similar spirals or, alternatively, you can design your own more complicated darning pattern.

Happy and useful stitching!

Rather than laboriously count threads, make light pencil dots at 1.5cm intervals (1). The first line of stitching takes up 2 threads of fabric at each dot (2). A change of colour and lines worked in step formation produces the pattern (3).

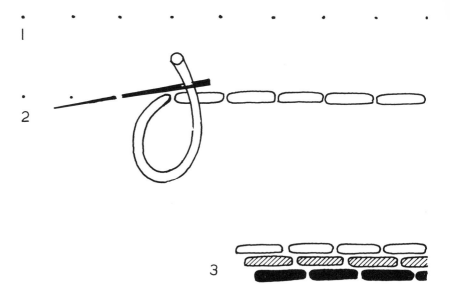

Other ideas relating to this pattern darning project

A child could easily manage the embellishment part of this design. If you cannot make the skirt for her, look out for a suitable straight-hemmed and recognisable-evenweave skirt in a chain store.
Buy another 40cm of fabric and make a long evening skirt.
Incorporate some gold or silver thread into the embellishment for a formal outfit.

12 Design an 'art' needlepoint *

I adapted a fascinating painting by modern artist Joshua May as a needlepoint. Now Joshua, who is five, is an experienced painter: his mother, though a talented dressmaker, has done little needlepoint before, but she enjoyed working up Joshua's design and following this simple formula below she can in future herself adapt her son's paintings.

It is so easy – and such fun – to design an original art needlepoint. Let me show you the simplest and least expensive method.

To design an art needlepoint you will need

An area of double canvas (the picture illustrated is worked on 10 Penelope, double canvas with 25 pairs of threads per 5cm, and the design was worked on an area 60 × 40cm)
An assortment of different-coloured wools (this picture could be worked in some of the attractive colours in DMC's 'Laine Colbert' range). This is a good chance to use up left-over embroidery and knitting threads!
Apart from the background colour, you will need an assortment of coloured felt markers or paints approximately the colours of your wools
Black NEPO pen
Tapestry needle (this design was worked with an 18)
A piece of paper exactly the size you would like your finished needlepoint to occupy
And a talented artist!

Joshua May drew this fascinating picture with felt markers (paper 29.5 × 40cm): his mother subsequently needlepointed the design.

First you catch the artist in a creative mood – you do not want him
to be temporarily destructive and tear the paper up or produce a
nightmare-like painting that you would not enjoy working! Give
him paper, and the markers or paints, and let him do exactly what
he likes. Find out what all the elements of his design are.

That is his role. Now you come in to play. Lay the finished painting
under your canvas and mark outlines of the motifs with your NEPO
pen. (If some of the colours are indistinct, outline the motifs on paper
so that they show through the canvas better.) Leave the NEPO to
dry, ideally for 24 hours.

Now you simply stitch the design, for you do have all the right
colours already to hand. This particular picture was completely
worked in basketweave tent stitch but you might like to incorporate
some other techniques into your work. Do not worry if some of the
NEPO marking shows outside a motif: it will be covered by the
background working.

See how easy it is to work your own art needlepoint! It would look
good if you had the two paintings, the original on paper and your
transposition on canvas, framed side by side – but alternatively you
might like to make the needlepoint into a knife-edge cushion (see
the next project).

To transpose a design (1), lay
a larger area of unworked
single or double canvas above
it (2) and mark the outline of
the design with NEPO pen (3).
If the background is to be
worked, the outline can be
linear as here. If,
alternatively, the background
of the design will be left
unworked, you should mark
the outline with dots at the
intersections of canvas
threads.

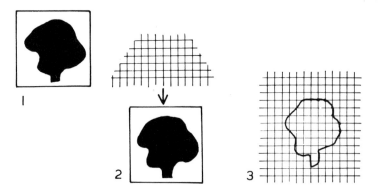

overleaf Both puppets are
embellished with appliqué
and full instructions are
given.

overleaf below Joshua May's
colourful picture was copied
by his mother on canvas and
subsequently made up into a
cushion. Why not use your
child's drawing for some 'art
needlepoint'?

overleaf opposite It is fun to
work embroideries specially
for children. This 'birth'
sampler is one of my designs
featured in the chapter on
cross stitch samplers.

Other ideas for designing needlepoints

You could ask each member of the family to design a picture in a
standard array of colours on papers to fit your dining room chairs.
You could then transpose all the designs to canvas – and your chairs
will be covered with individual seat designs, perhaps by those who
generally sit on the chairs.
Copy designs on wallpapers or curtain or other fabrics by the same
easy formula, namely laying unworked canvas directly on top.

13 ... and make it up *

It is difficult to find anyone to make up finished needlework – and sometimes much time and money is required anyway. So here is a simple method of doing it for yourself.

After Diana May had finished her picture (see the previous chapter), I blocked it for her. This means making the canvas straight and getting rid of any distortion. Diana was working in basketweave tent stitch, which does not distort much, and she was also working on double canvas, which generally keeps its shape. I therefore did not have as much of a problem as would have been the case had she been working in, say, continental tent stitch on single canvas.

My method of blocking does not require any professional equipment. If you have a proper blocking and stretching frame then you will probably already know how to use it.

To block needlework you will need

> A piece of fibreboard or hardboard which you have marked into a trellis of 2cm squares with a NEPO pen at least a week before (to make sure the ink has completely dried). The overall board should be at least 15cm bigger in each direction than the needlework
> Rustless pins or drawing pins
> A small hammer
> A damp towel (see below)

Lay the needlework on the towel and roll it in to a tube shape. Leave it for at least a couple of hours, and unwrap it.

Note: if you have any metal thread or embroidery threads that may possibly run a little, do not use this towel treatment. Go straight to the blocking and stretching described below.

Some people lay such techniques as needlepoint face down on a stretching board. I always lay any piece right way up. Not only can I then see the needlework while it is on the board but *just* in case my NEPO-marked trellis should run it marks only the reverse of the work.

Lay your piece, therefore, in the centre of the marked board and pin just outside the centre of the top of the stitched area to an intersection on the graph. The head of the pin should be facing away from the work. Gently pull down and pin just outside the centre of the bottom of the stitched area to the place on the board on which it lies flat, with no wrinkles and no undue pull.

Similarly pin just outside the centre of the left side and just outside the centre of the right side. Now back to the top of the work: pin about 2cm to the left of your first pin, then about 2cm to the right of your second, bottom pin, and so on, diametrically until you reach the corners.

As you pin make sure that your pins, and the edge of the finished area, are in alignment (the marked graph will help you). And make sure that all your pins face slightly out from the worked area.

opposite An unusual use for crewel embroidery: this project shows you how to produce an attractive mirror frame.

Iain Galloway wears his tie with stripes of drawn thread work through which the brilliant pink and navy silk lining provides contrast.

Diana May's cushion, worked from Joshua's drawing on p.63. The cushion has velcro fastening and a soft pillow pad inside. Joshua and his sister Olivia are playing with their appliqué puppets.

If you have enough pins fill in the gaps between your earlier pinnings: the more pins, the more exact will be your edging.

You should now leave the piece on the stretching board until it is completely dry, for several days at least. Ideally store it flat, and it should certainly be out of too much heat or light. Do not, under any circumstances, press it.

When you are quite sure it is dry you can remove all the pins.

You may now like to make the needlework up into a *knife edge pillow*.

For this you will need

Blocked needlework cut to 1cm surplus all around (if it is a fine needlework, also its area in lining fabric)

Its area in a suitable backing fabric

A strip of velcro 15mm wide to fit the bottom edge of the needlework

A similar length of bias (I used calico 5cm wide)

All-purpose thread to match the backing fabric and bias

Pillow pad to fit *or* 2 areas of calico slightly smaller than the finished needlwork and suitable amount of padding

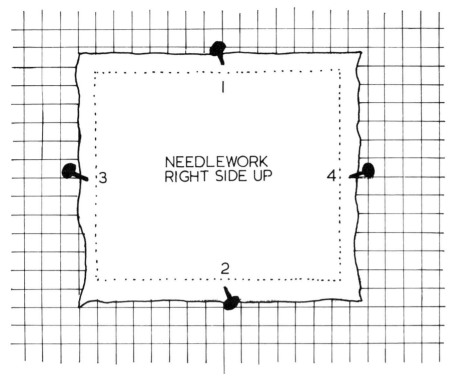

NEEDLEWORK
RIGHT SIDE UP

3

4

1

2

My blocking board is marked with 2cm squares. I lay a needlework right side up in the centre of the board and place pins first at the top, then bottom, then sides, just outside the worked area of the material. Subsequent pins follow in opposite pairs.

First sew 1 of the velcro parts to the bias, 1cm from the side. Hem the other long side of the strip. If you are working with, say, a fine silk needlepainting you should now tack it to the lining fabric.

Pin the base of the work to the side of the bias near the velcro, right side of the work to the velcro. Stitch exactly along the edge of the worked area (*always* stitch with the reverse of the embroidered material facing you rather than the lining, backing or whatever it is being joined to, as then you can more exactly place the stitches).

Stitch the other velcro part to the inside of what will be the base of your backing fabric. Place the backing fabric to the needlework, right sides together. Pin and stitch around both vertical and the top edges. Trim the excess surplus at the top 2 corners of the joined cushion and oversew the seam surpluses to prevent fraying.

Turn the pillow cover right sides out and tack around all round edges. *If*, and only if, it is a fabric and technique that you can iron (say blackwork), then carefully press 'knife edges'.

Remove the tackings and insert the pillow pad. The pillow will close with the velcro fastening.

If you are making your pillow pad you should join $3\frac{1}{2}$ sides of your 2 calico shapes leaving a central hole along one side. Turn the pillow pad cover with the seams inside, fill the cover with your chosen padding and stitch up the hole.

Other ideas for making up simple pillows

Add piping as in the small shadow-work cushion on p.131
Add a broderie anglaise ruffle. Place the gathered ruffle around the edges of the right side of the needlework, outside out, and then join the bias and the backing fabric in the usual way.

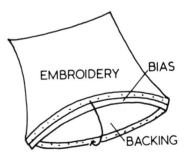

EMBROIDERY   BIAS

BACKING

When the cushion cover is finished, velcro (dotted) attached to the bias extending from the needlework folds over and meets the velcro attached to the inside open edge of the backing.

71

14 Drawn thread tie ******

Stripes of drawn thread work embellish this tie: stitching is bright pink to match the pink silk lining. Full instructions are given for making up the tie.

It is *so* difficult to find a really masculine present for a man who neither smokes nor plays golf (and there is no room in our house for any more books). I therefore designed this tie for my husband. Actually I cheated somewhat, in that I confiscated an old tie of his, took it to pieces and used it as a pattern, and then used some of the outside of that old tie as lining for this new one.

The tie is made of ecru hardanger cloth, with pairs of threads woven together. Decoration is provided by 2 stripes of drawn thread work stitched with bright pink stranded cotton to match the brilliant pink and navy silk lining.

To make a drawn thread tie like this you will need

> 60cm suitable fabric (I used ecru mercerised cotton evenweave hardanger with 50 pairs of threads per 5cm, fabric 107cm wide)
> Area of lining fabric at least 30 × 50cm (I cut the ends of the tie I was using as a pattern)
> 1 skein DMC stranded cotton (I used 602 bright pink, to complement my lining fabric)
> All-purpose sewing thread to suit your main fabric
> Tacking thread
> Blunt needle (I used tapestry 22)
> Ruler
> Tube turner
> Also, if your fabric needs it, a strip of bias to add weight and padding to the tie

First make 2 paper shapes and lay them on your main fabric. Indicate the outlines of the fabric shapes with tacking stitches but do not cut them out.

As its name implies, drawn thread work does have threads actually cut and carefully withdrawn. Now I suggest that you withdraw 2 stripes in the following way:

Lay the ruler centrally along the tie from the point of the larger (front) shape and pin 22cm from that point. Follow the pair of threads that you have pinned, diagonally up to the right and down to the left, and cut the threads 2cm in from either side of the shape. Carefully withdraw the threads between the 2 cuts.

Similarly cut the thread above it, and the one above that. Always making sure that your cuts are 2cm in from the sides of the shape, withdraw to this pattern:

stripe 1 – withdraw 4 pairs, leave 2 pairs, withdraw 4 pairs.

Now leave 10 pairs and withdraw another stripe as above.

Stitching was worked with 2 strands of my pink thread. Starting from the left, lower, end of the bottom of my first stripe I bound the bottom of the withdrawn area with hemstitch, worked so that I bound 3 pairs of remaining threads with stitches worked 3 pairs of threads down into the main fabric. When I finished along the bottom

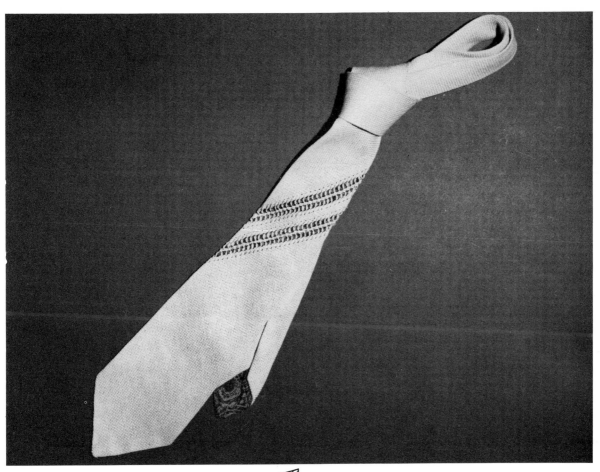

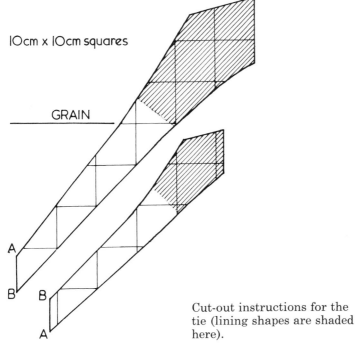

10cm x 10cm squares

GRAIN

A

B

B

A

Cut-out instructions for the tie (lining shapes are shaded here).

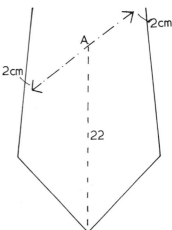

2cm

A

2cm

22

A is 22cm from the tip of the front tie shape. This thread is then followed diagonally up to the right and down to the left and small cuts made, 2cm in from the edges of the shape.

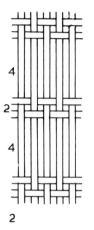

The thread is then withdrawn between cuts: each single thread shown here represents a pair of the hardanger threads used to make the tie in the photograph (1). The stripe formula is 4 threads withdrawn, 2 left and 4 withdrawn (2).

of the stripe, I turned the fabric through 180° and bound the other side of the stripe. The remaining pairs of threads in the centre of the stripe were then worked with double hemstitch. The other stripe was worked similarly.

To make up the tie

You should first make sure you have no untidy ends of embroidery threads visible from the front of the work.

Cut out tie linings. Lay the front lining on to the main fabric front shape, right sides of both fabrics up. Machine around the diagonal ends and 2 sides of the sandwich and turn it inside out so that the front side of the lining is visible through the holes of the embroidery. Tack.

Lay the back lining shape to the main fabric back shape, right sides together. Machine around the diagonal ends and 2 sides of the sandwich and turn it right sides out.

Join the tie together AB and press the seam open. Now fold the entire tie diagonally, end to end, right side in and machine from the front lining to the back lining. Turn the tie right side out with your tube turner and press. Continue the main seam by hand stitching main and lining shapes together as far down as you can.

Other ideas for this tie project

Work with appropriate coloured fabric and embroidery threads to produce a tie striped in your man's school, college or club colours. Cannibalise another tie to produce a template of a different shape. Use the same recipe I have given here to produce a bias-cut straight-ended cravat for a girlfriend.

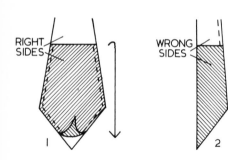

To make up the tie, front lining is placed on the main front, right sides up, and stitched. The shape is then turned (1). After the other tie end is attached to its lining, right sides together, and turned, and the two main shapes are joined AB, the tie is folded lengthwise right side in and stitched between linings. After it is turned (2) hand stitching can continue the seam past the lining.

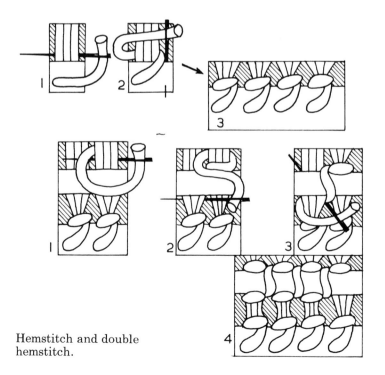

Hemstitch and double hemstitch.

15 Hardanger tray**

My mother-in-law's Christmas present this year is going to be a handy tray for passing round drinks or snacks.

I used a commercial tray kit with dark brown stained wood base and end handles. There is an inset oval with glass ready to receive a finished needlework. If you have a handyman in the house perhaps he could make you a similar tray (see the end of this chapter).

The inset needlework panel in this instance is a hardanger piece. A cutwork technique, hardanger is characterised by blocks of closely parallel satin stitches (read about hardanger in *The Coats Book of Embroidery*, p 122ff). Tradionally it is worked on special hardanger cloth, an evenweave with pairs of thread woven together. This piece is ecru hardanger and it is embellished with dark green pearl cotton 5. The cut holes reveal a backing to match the stain of the wood and threads remaining after holes have been cut are bound.

Wooden tray with hardanger panel inset behind glass – instructions are also given for making the tray (tray outside dimensions are 23.5 × 31cm).

To make a hardanger tray with needlework panel 18 × 25.5cm you will need

An area of hardanger cloth 25 × 35cm (I purchased 30cm of ecru mercerised cotton evenweave hardanger with 50 pairs of threads per 5cm, fabric 107cm wide)
Lining fabric 20 × 27cm
1 ball pearl cotton 5 (I used DMC 699 green)
Tapestry needle (I used tapestry 20)
Tray to mount your finished panel
Frame (I used my 20cm hoop)

First find the centre of your area of fabric and count your design from the centre of the paper graph here. Place the central area of fabric on the frame. Start with the main central diamond and work satin stitches from the paper pattern. You will see that satin stitches are worked over 4 threads and in this design all blocks are 5 threads wide. You are working blocks to form steps: notice how an adjacent riser and tread 'share' a hole of fabric. Try to work all your satin stitches from the *outside* of the motif in.

I found it easier to work all surface embroidery first, so when you have finished the central diamond, work all other satin stitching.

Then return to the central diamond. Using an extremely sharp pair of pointed scissors you cut any threads within the motif next to a satin-stitch block. Do not cut any threads at the 'ends' of blocks. Follow the diagram to make sure you cut away the right areas. After all cuts have been made carefully withdraw those threads so that you are left with a trellis.

I bound the trellis bars. You may prefer to needleweave the 4 threads of each bar.

Cut away the entire centre of the 2 motifs flanking the main central diamond: I left the centres of the 2 outer motifs but if you like you can cut yours away.

When all the embroidery is finished, carefully press the fabric from the reverse and mount it in the tray.

I hope my mother-in-law will use her present all year round – that is why I did not use Christmassy colours!

To make a wooden tray to mount this embroidery you will need

A handyman – or yourself – to prepare:

Wood 7mm thick, 2 side panels 4 × 31cm (outside measurements), with internal recess 1.2cm high, 4mm deep; 2 end panels 4 × 23.5cm (outside measurements), top rising to 6.5cm with cut-out for handle, recess as above
Glass 22.8 × 30.4cm
Wood 3mm thick 22.8 × 30.4cm with oval cut-out, maximum measurements 18.3 × 25.5cm
Hardboard 22.8 × 30.4cm
4 screws

The tray is constructed, and the needlework mounted as illustrated.

Other ideas relating to this project

Why not make a specifically Christmas tray, with cross-stitched holly? Adapt the hardanger motifs set out here to a small tablecloth.

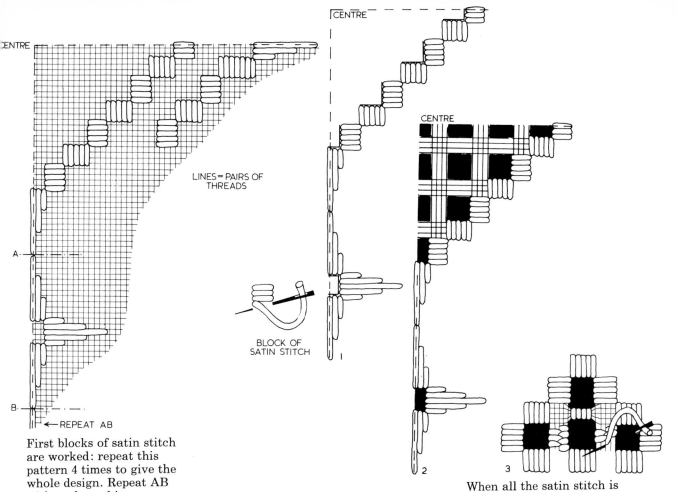

CENTRE

CENTRE

LINES = PAIRS OF
THREADS

A·

B·

←REPEAT AB

BLOCK OF
SATIN STITCH

CENTRE

1

2

3

First blocks of satin stitch
are worked: repeat this
pattern 4 times to give the
whole design. Repeat AB
with each working.

When all the satin stitch is
finished, the parts of the
inside of a motif that are
bordered by satin stitch are
cut as indicated (1 – fabric
threads not shown on this
drawing). Pair by pair those
threads are removed
altogether to leave a trellis
(2). Remaining threads can
be bound (horizontal bar) or
embellished with
needleweaving (vertical bars,
3).

Construction of a suitable
tray (measurements in
centimetres). The needlework,
with fabric backing behind,
is placed beneath the wooden
board with oval cut-out.
Glass, wood board,
needlework and hardboard
backing are inserted into the
recess of 3 sides of the tray.
The fourth side is fitted
accordingly and held with
screws.

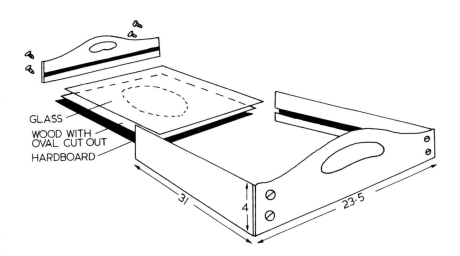

GLASS
WOOD WITH
OVAL CUT OUT
HARDBOARD

31

4

23.5

16 Hedebo sun visor **

I was fed up with hedebo table linens. I needed a sun visor (playing tennis in Caracas, at least, requires protection from that fierce sun!) and I wanted one to go with my tennis dress (see p 83) . . . so I designed and made this visor.

My sun visor is linen and the peak is embellished with a hedebo motif. The cut-out holes show especially well against a coloured lining. The adjustable strap of the visor fastens with velcro.

To make this hedebo sun visor you will need

> 30cm evenweave linen (I used Glenshee evenweave, ivory, 132cm wide)
> 20cm vilene heavy sew-in stiffener
> 20cm coloured lining (I used bright blue)
> 1 skein DMC coton-à-broder (I used 906 green)
> Tacking thread to match your coton-à-broder
> Ivory all-purpose thread
> 5cm white velcro, 1.5cm wide
> Pointed needle (I used crewel 4)
> Tracing paper and carbon
> Frame (I used my 10cm hoop)

Why should sun visors be boring? This has an attractive hedebo design on the peak.

First prepare paper pattern shapes, 1 for the peak (which will be used to make 2 fabric shapes) and 1 for the strap. Mark the outlines

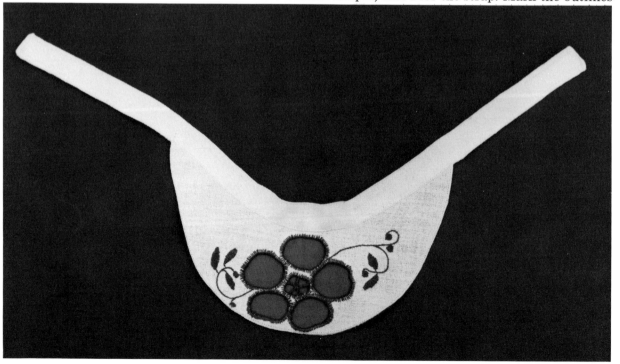

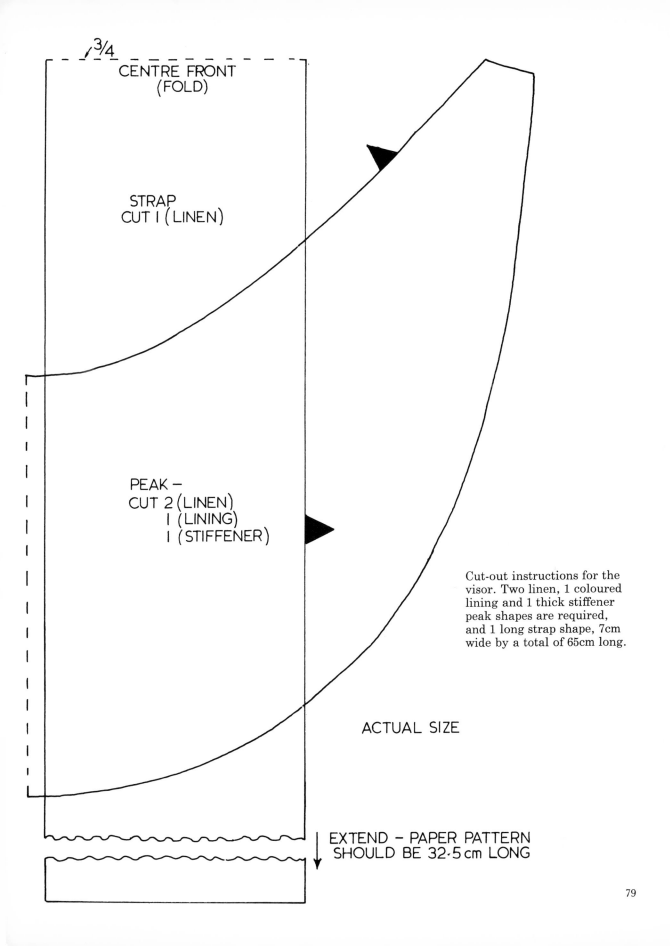

3/4

CENTRE FRONT
(FOLD)

STRAP
CUT 1 (LINEN)

PEAK —
CUT 2 (LINEN)
1 (LINING)
1 (STIFFENER)

Cut-out instructions for the
visor. Two linen, 1 coloured
lining and 1 thick stiffener
peak shapes are required,
and 1 long strap shape, 7cm
wide by a total of 65cm long.

ACTUAL SIZE

EXTEND – PAPER PATTERN
SHOULD BE 32·5 cm LONG

The embroidery motif should be sited in the middle of 1 of the linen peak shapes. All sections here marked 'X' will subsequently be cut and their edges bound with hedebo stitch.

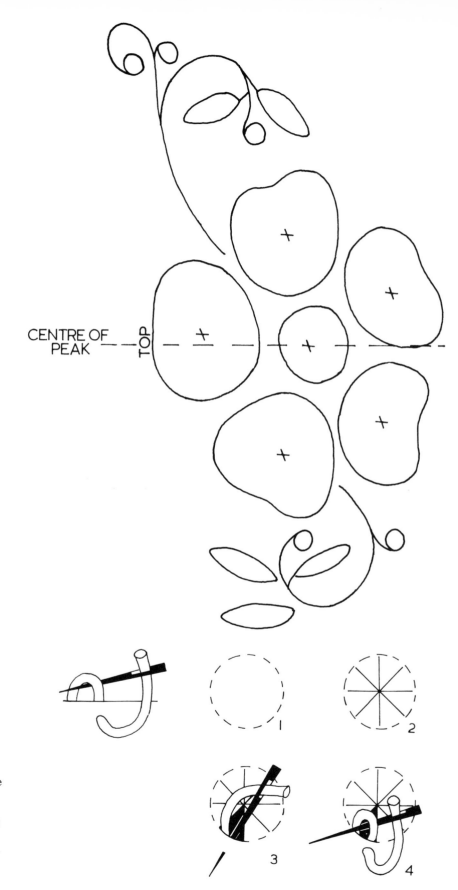

CENTRE OF PEAK — — TOP

Hedebo stitch (also known as hedebo buttonhole stitch). First an outline is covered by a line of running stitches (1), then radial cuts are made which almost reach to the running stitches (2). One by one the flaps are turned back as hedebo stitch is worked all around the hole (3 and 4).

of the shapes (2 peaks and 1 strap) on your linen with tackings but do not cut them out.

Transpose the embroidery design on to 1 of the linen peak areas, and place at least part of this area of the fabric on the frame. You will see that the flower petal areas will be removed. To work hedebo cut-outs first make little running stitches, in your tacking thread, around the marked edge of the section. Using sharp-pointed scissors you then make radial cuts almost – but not quite – to that peripheral stitching. These flaps are turned back one by one and hedebo button-hole stitch is worked around the entire hole.

From the reverse of the linen, surplus fabric flaps can be carefully cut away after a hole is bound. When all the holes have been worked in this way, the central hole can be further embellished by radial buttonhole bars.

Stems are worked in stem stitch. Leaves and buds are closely parallel satin stitch.

When all the embroidery is worked, remove the frame and cut out the 3 linen shapes (2 peaks and 1 strap). Cut also 1 peak shape from lining fabric and 1 from stiffener.

Tack together a sandwich of embroidered linen peak (right side up), lining and stiffener. Place this sandwich with the other linen, right sides together, pin, tack and machine around the longer curved side.

Make small V cuts in the surplus to accommodate the extra fabric, and turn the peak right sides out. Tack around the longer curved side of the peak and machine stitch as close to the edge as possible.

Place the strap above the embroidered side of the peak, matching notches, and machine the shorter curve of the peak to the strap. Now fold the entire strap lengthwise, the seam attaching the peak to the strap facing in. Machine stitch along all the rest of the length of the strap (that is to say, to either side of the attachment to the peak, as far as the ends of the strap) and stitch along both end edges. Trim the surplus corners, and turn the two strap 'arms' right side out.

Turn under the remaining strap surplus and neatly hem it to the peak, just covering the machine line where the peak has already been attached to the strap.

Tack around the entire perimeter of the strap and machine stitch as close to the edge as possible. Stitch one of the velcro strips to the right side of one end of the strap, and the other to the wrong side of the other end of the strap.

Now, who's for tennis?

Other ideas for this hedebo design

Work the same design in DMC gold or silver embroidery thread on white linen and place it against a gold or silver lining to make a disco visor.

If you really want more table linen, work the hedebo motif diagrammed here in each corner of a table cloth and once on each of a set of napkins.

Form more complicated hedebo bars and 'rings' (see *The Coats Book of Embroidery* p 130ff).

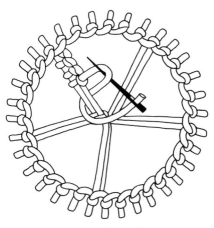

When all the cut holes have thus been bound, you can work radial bars in the central hole. Long stitches are taken across the hole and these 'bars' are bound with hedebo stitch.

The peak (shaded) is stitched to 1 long side of the strap, right sides together (1). The arms of the strap are stitched, right sides together (2). The arms are turned the right way out and the remaining raw edge of strap side is brought over the peak join, turned neatly under and hemmed.

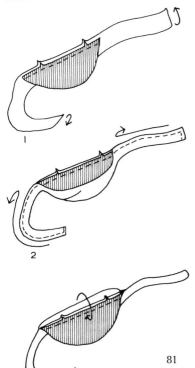

17 Knot-initialled tennis dress **

I wanted a practical and reasonable tennis dress with a couture look – hence this outfit! It is made up in cotton seersucker with green, blue and white vertical stripes 1.8cm wide. There are 6 pieces to the dress and at the front of the neck is a large initial worked in close french knots. The colour of the stitching changes from blue to white to accommodate the change of fabric colour.

In this instance I worked the initial first and then made up the item (no particular reason except that I find knotting complicated to manage if I have too much fabric to handle).

To make this dress (suitable for size 8 through 12) you will need

> 1.70m suitable fabric 90cm wide (I used a cotton seersucker from John Lewis)
> 2 skeins DMC stranded cotton (I used 1 each white and 797 blue)
> All-purpose thread to suit your fabric
> 48cm zipper for the back seam opening
> Pointed needle (I used crewel 4)
> Tracing paper and carbon
> Small frame (I used my 10cm hoop)

First you should enlarge the diagrams here to form paper patterns. If you are size 12 add 5mm around all edges. If you are size 8 take off 5mm around all edges.

Cut out your fabric shapes. You should have: 2 × back, 2 × side back, 2 × side front, 1 × front, 2 × armhole facing, 1 × front neck facing and 2 × back neck facing.

Put all the shapes except for the main front carefully to one side. Choose which initial you will stitch (you can enlarge it if you like – I doubled the size of my 'M'). Trace your required initial on to the centre of the front panel. The top of the initial should be 3cm below the top edge of the shape. Remove tracing paper and carbon and place an appropriate area of fabric on your frame.

I stitched entirely with *3 strands* of embroidery thread. Since it is difficult to maintain equal tension when 'knotting' I personally prefer to sew with a shorter length than usual.

First mark the outline of each part of the initial with running stitches to provide a 'back up' if your subsequent knots do not provide a neat outline. Then start working knots around, just outside these markings. Now infill, in whatever order you like (start from one end, work haphazardly and so on) until all the area is completely filled. Change from one colour to another when you reach a different coloured 'stripe'. When you have finished, remove the frame and prepare to make up the dress.

To make up the tennis dress

You should first tack all seams and try it on – even if you have

Who's for tennis? This dress – for which full instructions are given – is personalised with an elaborate knotted monogram below the front of the neck.

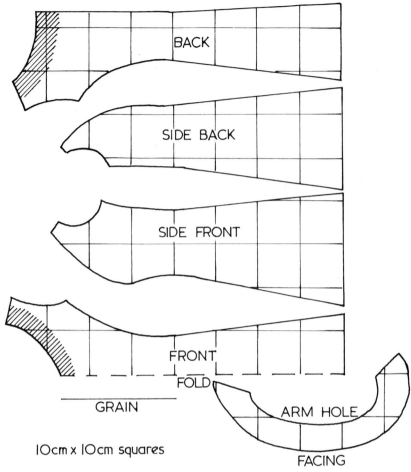

BACK

SIDE BACK

SIDE FRONT

FRONT

FOLD

GRAIN

10cm x 10cm squares

ARM HOLE

FACING

already altered the basic pattern size from, say, 10 to 12 you might still have to make the seams narrower. When you think you have achieved perfect fit you can proceed to final stitching. First stitch the 2 back panels together, joining them along their shared seam from a measurement of 49cm from the top to the hem of the garment.

Put the zip in the prepared gap.

Now stitch all other long vertical seams – make sure you gather the surplus at the bust conveniently to fit the front panel to the 2 side front pieces.

Press all your main seams and stitch the shoulder seams. Join the armhole facings, one end to the other, and think about the edging that you would like to use.

I used facings (see pattern). You might prefer bias braid or machine stitching. I joined the front facing to the curved ends of the back facing and pinned the facing to the neck of the garment, right sides together. Then I stitched, pressed and made small Vs to accommodate curves. I turned the dress right side out and machine stitched as close to the edge as I could.

I attached the armhole facings to the armholes, right sides together and facing seam corresponding to the join of the 2 side panels. I stitched, made small Vs and turned the dress right side out before machining close to the edge.

A versatile housecoat that can be worn by day or night – its broderie anglaise decoration shows especially well when it is worn over a dark garment. Mary Gostelow is holding a freeform bargello picture.

This bright 4-way bargello panel was made up into a typewriter cover with a skirt that can be removed for washing.

Two smaller items that would make lovely presents: a practical and washable cover for a camera and a small box embellished with a couched pre-Columbian motif.

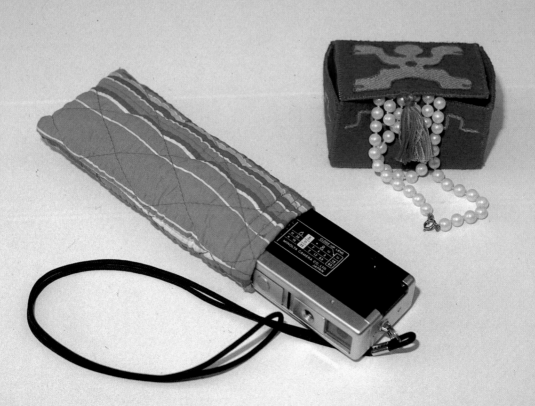

A trio of needlepoint tops! Mary Gostelow, wearing a tabard with a bright floral front, holds a man's waistcoat worked in 'Chottie's plaid' design while Joanna Sale wears her dress with canvas insert.

A miniature king, fashioned around a wooden clothes peg, is mostly worked with tent stitch, bargello and the fascinating 'tyler rose' stitch. He is 12cm high in his crown and brown shoes.

A B C D E F G H
I J K L M N O P
R S T U V W Y Z

French knot.

Alphabet possibilities. You can enlarge if you like, using the enlarging method given in the Introduction.

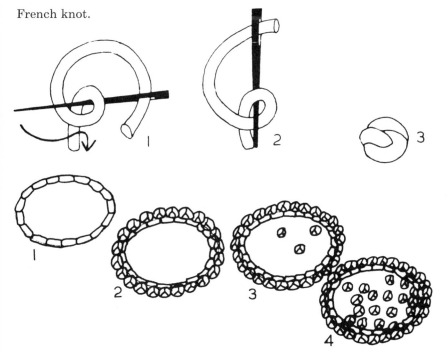

My method of infilling with knots is first to outline an area with running stitches (1), work french knots just outside those stitches (2) and infill at random (3, 4) until all is filled and the running stitches are covered.

You will notice that there is only 1cm hem allowance on my paper pattern. I turned the small surplus back and under, and machine stitched around.

It all sounds so simple writing the instructions for this dress. I hope you enjoy making it – and then showing it off on the court!

Other ideas relating to this project

Leave the 2 back panels of the dress open, attach ties, and make an initialled housecoat or uniform jacket.

Make the dress all in white and initial it in a bright colour.

opposite The cut of this full-length kaftan was copied from a garment bought in an open market on the Ivory Coast. Mary Gostelow's version has a large Mexican sun motif embroidered on the front in metal thread.

18 Machine-stitched blanket cover *

One of those little niceties of life that Americans seem to take as a matter of course are blanket covers, usually in seersucker or a similar lightweight fabric, in a colour to match the bedroom decor and lavishly decorated with white lace, often including the monogram of the lady of the house. Such covers are put over blankets when the bed is made up, and are revealed when the main coverlet or bedspread is taken off before going to bed.

I made blanket covers for our guest-room beds. My covers are green batiste embroidered in dark brown to match my colour scheme. The covers are machine washable and do not crease.

To make blanket covers you will need (for each single bed)

> 4m of lightweight fabric at least 90cm wide (I used Jonelle batiste)
> All-purpose thread to match
> Another all-purpose thread for your stitching (I used dark brown Gutermanns)
> 'Invisible' pen
> Frame (I used my 10cm hoop)
> Sewing machine (I worked with my Frister + Rossmann Cub 4)

Decorated blanket cover for the guest bed has its own machine-stitched message; nightdress by Julius Garfinckel & Co.

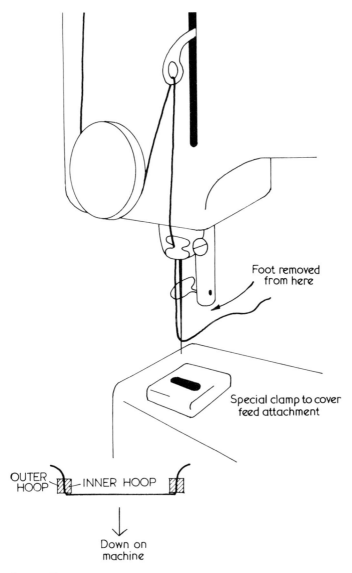

Foot removed
from here

Special clamp to cover
feed attachment

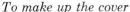

OUTER
HOOP — INNER HOOP

↓

Down on
machine

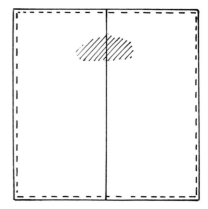

The cover is formed of 2
lengths of fabric 2m
long joined and hemmed all
around. The stitched message
(shaded) should be 25cm from
the top of the cover.

Before any embroidery is done,
the foot is removed from the
machine and a special clamp,
usually supplied in the
accompanying toolbox, is
fitted over the feed
mechanism.

(Drawing in cross-section)
If a thick thread is being
used, it should be wound, by
hand if necessary, on the
underneath spool and a
thinner thread passed through
the needle's eye. Fabric on a
frame lies on the machine's
base under the needle.

To make up the cover

Divide your fabric into 2 × 2m lengths, stitch one to the other,
joining selvedge to selvedge right sides together. Press the seam
open. Make a narrow hem around all 4 edges of the cover.

With your pen you can now write your inscription in the upper
centre of the cover, right side up (the top of your message should be
about 25cm from the top of the cover).

Before you embroider you should familiarise yourself with your
particular machine's feed control. On the Cub 4, for instance, I was
instructed to lower a small lever which lowered the feed dogs. On
some other machines a little clamp, supplied in the tool box, covers
the feed.

Unscrew the presser foot and remove it: you will stitch with a
naked needle so you have to be particularly aware of your hands!
Thread your coloured thread through the needle and on to the
bobbin.

Place a suitable part of your design, right side up, on the hoop with the sides of the hoop rising *above* the fabric (that is to say, the outer hoop goes under the fabric and the inner hoop above it). Carefully slide the frame under the needle.

I worked with a straight stitch set at medium length. First I brought my bobbin thread end up through the fabric so that I could control both thread ends. I found that caution pays when starting decorative machine stitching: I tried one or two stitches until I got hold of the fact that to move the direction of stitching to the *left* I – and not the machine – had to move the frame to the *right*.

It is a good idea to work back and forth over the same line of the design to give a solid 'cover'. Make sure you stop and start with each new letter.

When you have finished all the stitching, immerse the design in cold water and the blue lines will disappear.

Other ideas for this project

After you have finished your decorative stitching, apply lace around it and to cover all seams and hems.

If you really enjoy machine embellishment you could buy lengths of sheeting and make up your own monogrammed linens.

The frame is set beneath the needle and one stitch is taken to pull the thread from the underneath spool through the fabric. The frame is held in both hands and the embroiderer is ready to begin.

below Pulling the frame slowly to the *right* produces stitches moving in a *left* direction.

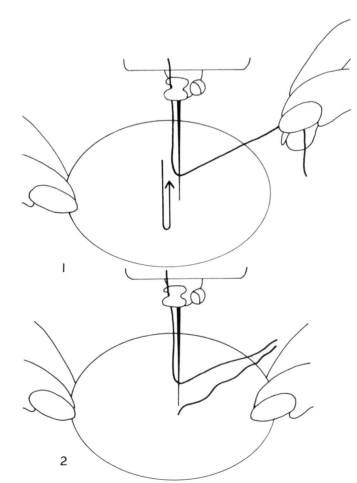

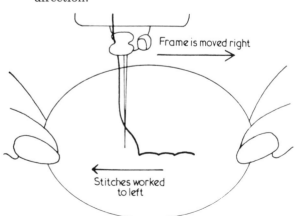

19 Metallic kaftan **

In a market in Abidjan some years ago I bought a tie-dye dress, full length and with striking cut-outs beneath both arms.

Finally, after many tries which made the complexities of trouser seam constructions seem like pre-school play, I did manage to fathom out how my dress was put together. Here is the pattern to share with you.

The kaftan fits any size and is one of those anywhere, anytime garments. The front and back of the kaftan are the same shape but below the neck of what becomes the front of the garment is a sun design adapted from an ancient Mexican design.

I made my kaftan in shocking pink seersucker and embroidered it with DMC semi-fine gold embroidery thread: it is completely *machine washable* in temperatures up to 45°C (113°F)!

To make this gold-embroidered kaftan you will need

    2.60m of lightweight fabric at least 108cm wide (I used a John Lewis seersucker)
    1 reel DMC semi-fine gold embroidery thread
    All-purpose sewing thread to match your fabric
    Pointed needle (I used crewel 5)
    Tracing paper and dressmaker's carbon
    Frame (I used my 10cm hoop)

First make a paper pattern from the diagram illustrated. Fold the fabric in half, across the grain, and then in half again, selvedge to selvedge, and cut out from the paper pattern.

Because you are working with one piece of fabric you will find it easier *to make the dress up* before you embroider.

Lay the front and back of the dress together, right sides out, and stitch around both armholes. Now comes the only complicated part. You cannot turn the dress 'inside out' but you can feel, first from the sleeve and then from inside the body part, to the inside of both these seams. Pull to the inside enough fabric to make a french seam, pin and stitch (you will find you have to do it in two stages, first from the sleeve and then from the body part). Snip your french seam almost to the stitching to accommodate the fabric around the curves.

Both sleeves are stitched in this manner. Then you turn back and hem all side edges and both hem edges of the garment. Turn back and hem around the neck. Lastly, with the garment still right side out, stitch both seams AB from beneath the sleeve cut-outs to the hem.

When your garment is made up you can *embroider the sun*. Trace the motif on to your tracing paper, and apply it with the 'trace and carbon' method to the upper yoke of the garment so that the top of the outline is about 3cm from the neck. Remove the tracing paper and carbon and place a suitable area of the fabric on your frame.

All the embroidery will be worked with the gold thread which is

The idea for this kaftan with cut-outs under both sleeves came from an Abidjan market: the brilliant pink seersucker robe is embellished with a gold sun design adapted from a Mexican motif.

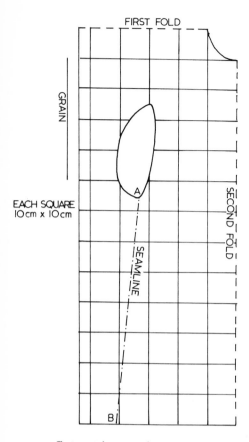

Cut-out instructions.

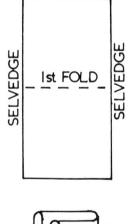

A single length of fabric is folded twice.

supple and extensible, although it does sometimes 'catch' and the outer coating of the thread may tear if you sew with too long a length. It is difficult to knot this thread and I found it easier to begin a new length with 1 or 2 small back stitches on the line along which I was subsequently going to sew.

Most of the embroidery is chainstitch. Outline all the sun's rays and the outermost circle with chainstitch. Work long straight stitches in zigzag formation from the central to the innermost circles before working chainstitch around both those circles too. Eyes can be infilled with parallel vertical straight stitches about 2mm apart before chainstitch is worked around the outlines and large eyelashes, in pairs of straight stitches, formed above each eye.

Finished . . . and what an attractive garment to wear to so many places!

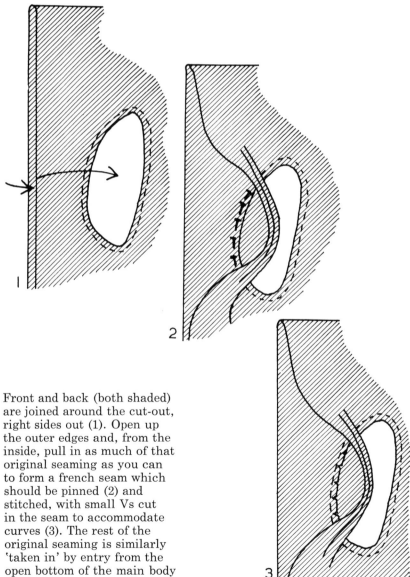

Front and back (both shaded) are joined around the cut-out, right sides out (1). Open up the outer edges and, from the inside, pull in as much of that original seaming as you can to form a french seam which should be pinned (2) and stitched, with small Vs cut in the seam to accommodate curves (3). The rest of the original seaming is similarly 'taken in' by entry from the open bottom of the main body of the robe.

94

A

B

A JOIN TO MAIN MOTIF B

Motif outline.

The outlines are all worked in chainstitch. Straight stitches connect the two inner circles and vertical straight stitches partly fill the eye. Pairs of straight stitches form eyelashes.

Other ideas relating to this kaftan project

Instead of stitching with a metal thread you might like to couch a thicker metal that cannot itself be taken through the fabric. You should couch this metal with another thread, and take the ends of the thick metal thread through a prepared hole by 'plunging', also known as 'sinking'.

Why not use two lengths (each 1.30m long) of fabric to form a different coloured back and front to your kaftan? Stitch the sun on one half and design a moon shape for the other.

Extend the sun design given here to form a fake chain around the neck of the kaftan.

20 Needlepaint your 'home town' ***

By 'needlepainting' I mean using needle and thread as brush and paint. Stitches are worked not with regard to technique or stitch length but, rather, to simulate brush strokes.

I love needlepainting, for it is satisfying to 'build up' a picture. Sometimes layers of 'stitches' are worked one on top of the other.

The little picture illustrated here is a view of the village street in Milton Abbas, Dorset, where I live. You will note that areas of fabric have intentionally not been covered with stitching. I deliberately tried to give a feeling of perspective and depth to my picture.

If you have never done any needlepainting before I suggest you start with a 'local view', instructions for which are outlined below. Later you will find that you can progress with confidence to needlepainting objects and even people.

To do a local view needlepainting you will need

> An area of fabric (I actually worked on evenweave linen but I think you would find white satin or a cotton batiste preferable. You will need *at least* 10cm more than the measurements of your finished picture: I worked with an area 30 × 30cm to produce a picture 6.5 × 16cm)
> As large a selection of DMC stranded cottons as you have available
> Tacking thread
> A pointed needle (I found a sharp 8 best)
> Photograph of the view that you want to needlepaint, same size as your intended picture
> Tracing paper and carbon
> Frame large enough to accommodate your whole picture (I used my 20cm hoop)

Lay the tracing paper above the photograph and trace *main* outlines of your view: there is no need to mark small windows or any shading.

Transfer these outlines to your fabric using the usual tracing paper and carbon method. Remove both papers and place the fabric on the frame.

You will need the fabric held as taut as possible throughout. You may, indeed, frequently have to tighten it.

I suggest you first go over your carbon outlines with long tackings. At this stage learn the technique of not worrying about stitch length or whether or not you are piercing a thread of fabric or going between two threads. Concentrate on what you want your stitch to do. Because you are worrying only about the front of your work you can knot thread ends and take long strides, on the back of your work, from one side of your fabric to the other. Try if you can never to turn over: work continuously from the right side of the fabric.

When your tackings are all worked you can begin the main stitching. I find it easier to work recessed areas first – in the case of the Milton Abbas picture I started with the background hills. Thread

opposite A needlepainted view of an English village worked throughout in 1 strand of DMC stranded cottons (finished picture 6.5 × 16cm). Full instructions are given for designing and working *your* local view.

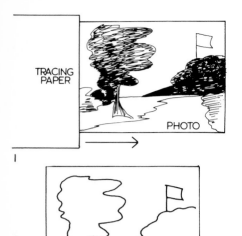

Lay tracing paper over a photograph the same size as your intended picture (1) and trace main outlines (2).

up a not-too-long length of a suitable colour and start covering the area with stitching. You will probably work mostly in straight stitches. Make the stitch direction suitable to your picture.

It is better not to do enough stitching than to do too much (it is easier to put on 'another layer' than to undo).

When you think you have finished an area progress to another area. Make stitches suitable to that part of your picture. I worked my thatch in many closely parallel vertical stitches. As contrast tiles were formed from horizontal stitches.

Trees should be worked trunks first and greenery after. Straight stitches in higgledy-piggledy disarray can simulate foliage – so also can a mass of french knots.

You will probably find, in fact, that satin and straight stitches, french knots and perhaps buttonhole stitch (for fences) are the only 'techniques' employed. But try not to think of them as such. When you need a knotty 'brush stroke' then make a knot.

Leave highlights – outlines of houses, windows and so on – until last. When you *think* you have finished put your work to one side – say for a day – and then come back to it.

Look at the picture critically. Does it need more substance? Is too much of the fabric left unworked? Would it help to add a hint of sunlight by outlining distant hills in golden stitching?

Is any of the original tacking showing? If so, take it out.

And when you have finally finished, *what* a lovely picture you should have. People will wonder how you did it . . . and did *you* know you were such a good needlepainter?

Other ideas relating to this project

Work a picture *en grisaille*, that is to say in shades of grey and black and white. Much more concentration is required for shading.

If you are happy with your needlepainting why not have it photographed for a Christmas card?

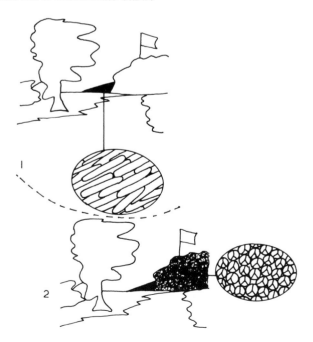

After the outlines are transposed to fabric they are tacked. With needlepainting recessed areas are 'painted' first. Here a far hillside has been worked with straight stitches not necessarily exactly parallel or equidistant one from another but giving an overall effect of the slope (1). French knots can be used for a bushy hillside or tree (2).

21 Needlepoint tops for all the family **

Here is a trio for your family! The man's waistcoat has a smart tartan front, the lady's tabard looks stunning over a dress or long trousers, and the little girl's dress features her own initial.

I made my pieces from lock thread (interlock) cotton canvas which does not distort. You may, however, prefer to use new lightweight plastic canvas. If you then stitch with a washable knitting yarn and make the rest of the garment in a washable fabric, the whole piece can be laundered at home.

When making any garment with canvas inserts it is a good idea to do all the dressmaking first and then decorate the canvas, making sure that all ends of needlepoint yarn are 'hidden' in edge bindings wherever possible.

Here are instructions for making my three garments.

For the man's waistcoat you will need
(For details of sizing, and how to enlarge a garment, see the Introduction.)

> 60cm lock thread canvas, 28 pairs of threads per 5cm
> 60cm fabric for back of waistcoat (I used black needlecord)
> 2 cards bias binding to match back fabric
> 1 reel all-purpose thread, to match back fabric
> 18 tapestry needle
> Wools for your tartan: I used 2oz each Appletons tapestry wool 310–6 dark olive; 690–3 honeysuckle; 840–1 heraldic gold; 1oz each Appletons tapestry wool 940–7 bright rose pink; 993 black

First, follow the paper pattern and cut out 1 fabric back panel and 2 canvas fronts. Join side and shoulder seams and press open. Bind all exposed edges of garment with bias binding.

Now decide what manly pattern you want to work. I decided on a 'McGostelow' plaid using 'Chottie's plaid', developed by Chottie Alderson (explained in detail on p 180 of *The Coats Book of Embroidery*). First I worked vertical rows of alternate half-cross stitches. Then I turned the panel through 90° and worked similar rows of alternate half-cross stitches, filling in the gaps and always sticking to my prepared colour formula: 2 rows 940–7; 6 rows 690–3; 2 rows 993; 6 rows 310–6; 6 rows 840–1.

For the lady's tabard you will need

> 50cm lock thread canvas, 24 pairs of threads per 5cm
> 50cm fabric for back of tabard (I used powder blue needlecord)
> 2 cards bias binding to complement back fabric
> 1 reel all-purpose thread, same colour as binding
> 18 tapestry needle
> NEPO marker

Wools for your tabard front: I used 2oz Appletons tapestry wool 740–6 bright china blue; 1oz each Appletons tapestry wool 740–2 paler china blue; 550–1 bright yellow; 550–3 brighter yellow; 550–7 orange shade of bright yellow; 420–6 leaf green

First cut out canvas front piece and fabric back panel. Sew the shoulder seams together and press open. Bind neck and side seams. Then bind waists of front and back panels, leaving 50cm extra binding each side. Fold these surplus lengths in half lengthwise, sew and seal ends (these will form waist ties).

Now design your canvas panel. If you like you can follow my bright-flower design. Mark the outlines with NEPO marker and then stitch in basketweave tent stitch. I finished off by working radial lines as 'stamens' for some flowers: make sure that all such radial stitches emanate from the circumference and work towards the hub, and weave threads in and out on the reverse of the canvas.

opposite Mary Gostelow wears the canvaswork tabard. Joanna Sale wears her initialled dress. Bill Alderson holds a man's waistcoat that is being embellished with 'Chottie's plaid', named after his famous needlepointer wife: only one side of the waistcoat has been worked with its final cross-hatching.

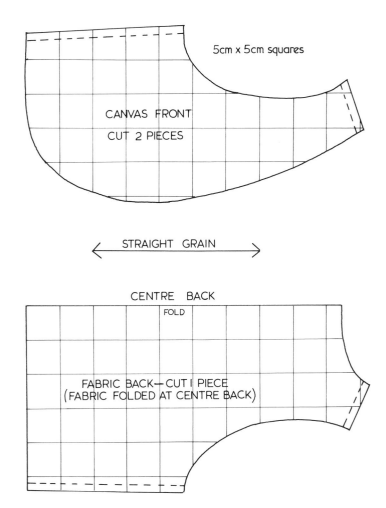

5cm x 5cm squares

CANVAS FRONT
CUT 2 PIECES

STRAIGHT GRAIN

CENTRE BACK
FOLD

FABRIC BACK—CUT 1 PIECE
(FABRIC FOLDED AT CENTRE BACK)

Cutting details for man's waistcoat.

Cutting details for woman's tabard.

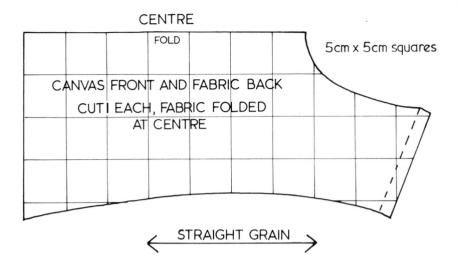

CENTRE

FOLD

CANVAS FRONT AND FABRIC BACK

CUT I EACH, FABRIC FOLDED AT CENTRE

5cm x 5cm squares

STRAIGHT GRAIN

On the canvas front of your tabard you might like to draw a large abstract floral design as shown. Whatever design you choose should cover all the canvas.

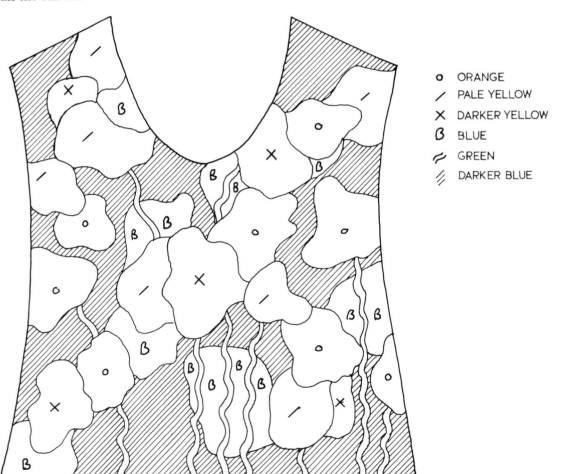

o   ORANGE
/   PALE YELLOW
X   DARKER YELLOW
ß   BLUE
~   GREEN
/// DARKER BLUE

For the girl's pinafore dress you will need
(Note: the paper pattern fits a 4-year-old. You may prefer to use another pinafore pattern, or you can add extra fabric or make larger seams to accommodate a different-sized child.)

120cm fabric 90cm wide (I used green sailcloth)
30cm zip, same colour as fabric
2 cards bias binding, same colour as fabric
1 reel all-purpose thread, same colour as fabric
20cm lock thread canvas with 28 pairs of threads per 5cm
18 tapestry needle
NEPO marker
Wools for the canvas panel: I used 1oz each Paternayan
tapestry wool 865; 839; 559
Dinner plate not more than 20cm diameter

Follow the paper pattern and cut out 1 front and 2 back fabric panels. Using your dinner plate as guide, cut a circle of canvas and lay it on the *wrong* side of the centre of the front panel. Pin and tack, and machine zigzag all around the edge of the canvas, holding it to the fabric. Working from the front of the fabric, carefully remove the fabric inside the machined 'circle' so that the canvas behind is revealed.

Now decorate the canvas. I drew Joanna's initial with NEPO marker and worked it in pale pink basketweave tent stitch. Then I filled in the rest of the canvas area with vertical stripes of green and darker pink basketweave stitch.

Now sew up the centre back seam of the pinafore as far as where the bottom of the zip will be. Press. Insert zip. Sew up shoulder and main side seams and press. Bind all revealed edges, including hem, with bias tape.

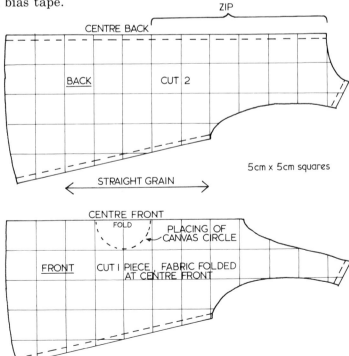

Cutting details for girl's dress.

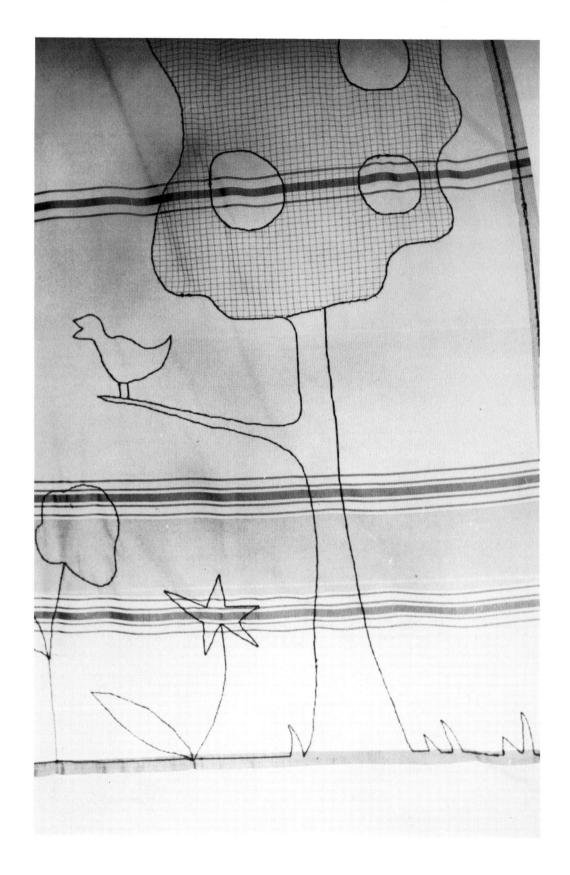

22 Net curtain with a difference *

Especially when you live on a main street net curtains are sometimes necessary – and those that you can buy are often boringly impersonal.

I have designed this net-curtain-with-a-difference so that it adds decoration to its main purpose. You can use your own creativity to design a curtain or you can follow my instructions and work a similar bird-on-a-tree pattern.

opposite Why not stitch an *attractive* net curtain? This piece is stitched in white threads and measures 115 × 68cm.

To make my net curtain you will need

1 area of net (I used 70cm of nylon net 115cm deep, with its own 5cm hem and woven with patterned stripes)
2 balls DMC pearl cotton size 5, white
1 reel DMC brilliant machine embroidery twist, white
2 blunt needles (I used tapestry 20 and 24)
'Invisible' pen
Frame (I used my 20cm hoop)

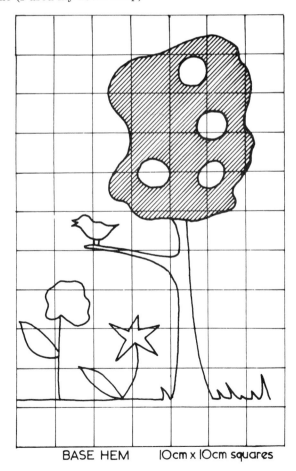

BASE HEM   l0cm x l0cm squares

Pattern diagram for the curtain (the pattern does not extend right to the top of the fabric).

No surplus threads must show through an unworked area. When you have to start a new thread, make a few back stitches from the direction in which you will subsequently stitch (1). Then stitch over those back stitches and continue along your way (2).

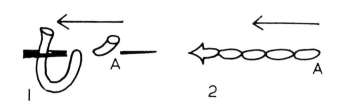

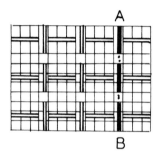

Part of the tree is infilled. Pairs of threads are stitched to form a trellis: stitches work over 2, under 2 net threads and rows are 4 net threads apart. One black row AB helps to clarify this.

With the net that is intended for curtains you generally work sideways on, with the selvedges horizontally at the top and bottom of your curtain. Turn back the sides of your curtain and 'hem' with chainstitch in pearl cotton on your bigger needle.

Follow the directions for enlarging the diagram here and lay your net above your large pattern. Pin it to the paper, and outline the design on the net with your invisible pen. Remove the paper and place an appropriate part of the net on the frame.

You must remember that with net embroidery no surplus threads, knots, etc, must be outside your finished stitching. You should therefore start all your embroidery threads by working a few minute back stitches along the invisible-pen line along which you are shortly going to work. Finish threads similarly.

The entire outline design will be worked with pearl cotton double running stitch. Each of my stitches is about 5mm long, over 3 net threads.

When you have finished outlining you can infill some of the motifs with machine twist on the smaller needle. Here you can see how the main tree has been infilled with a trellis of double thicknesses of machine twist worked in horizontal and vertical rows of running stitch over 2 net threads, rows 4 net threads apart.

The completed curtain can be dipped in cold water to remove the blue line – and you are ready to hang your 'art work'.

Other ideas for this net project

Stitch, in various colours, the letters of the alphabet on a curtain for a child's room.
Draw a full-length palm for a net curtain for a doorway.
Use the design illustrated here for a hostess apron made of finer-quality net.
Draw a pattern of roses and other flowers and embroider a wedding veil of bridal-quality net.

23 Patchwork jacket **

I was staying with a dear friend in sunny California when I first came across 'California jackets'. These are gorgeous needlework *pièces de résistance* and many women have several, each in a different colour scheme. One jacket might be mostly reds, another all colours of the rainbow and yet another in an assortment of lurex and other evening fabrics.

All the jackets are formed of large patches of different fabrics and masses of braids and ribbons. Sometimes they are further embellished with surface embroidery. The jackets are usually simply cut, with straight sleeves and no collar or fastening. They are lightly quilted and reversible.

I could not wait to make myself a jacket in 'California style' and I purchased a variety of bright cotton fabrics right there in Redondo Beach. I started sewing as soon as I reached home.

To make a 'California style' patchwork jacket you will need

> A jacket pattern, preferably a simple cut with no darts or gathers. I used a Halston design, McCall's 6528, and I omitted the collar
> Enough fabric to make the jacket, plus 50cm (my pattern called for 2.5m of cotton 1.20m wide so I bought 3m). This 'main' fabric will be the lining of the jacket: the extra 50cm is for bias for the edges
> The same amount of vilene light sew-in less the extra 50cm (I bought 2.5m)
> A generous supply of lightweight fabrics and lengths of braids and ribbons in your chosen colour scheme (I used apple green, bright pink, black and white)
> 3m plain satin ribbon, about 1.5cm wide, in a colour complementary to the lining fabric
> All-purpose sewing thread in a colour that will show least on the lining fabric
> Embroidery threads as required

To make your jacket

First cut out pattern pieces in the main fabric and vilene (do not cut out facings). Tack the vilene to the back of the fabric shapes and lay them on a flat surface, vilene side up.

There are now two 'patching routes' that you can follow. Both share the same final making-up instructions.

Patching route A

This is the method that I used. It is quick and produces sometimes large and irregularly shaped patches.

Prepare an assortment of pairs of 'patches' from your fabrics. You can embroider some if you like. Do not turn the edges under. Pin them in a jigsaw all over the vilene shapes. Remember to try for

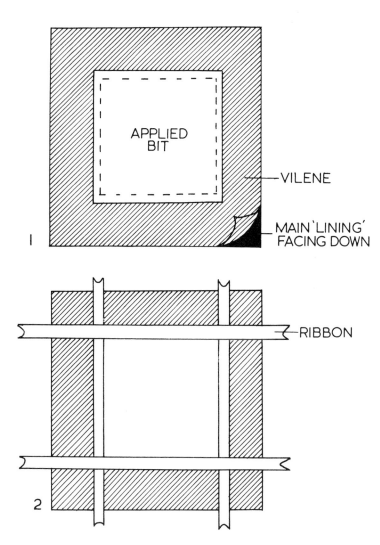

APPLIED
BIT

VILENE

MAIN 'LINING'
FACING DOWN

1

RIBBON

2

opposite This 'California style' patchwork jacket was great fun to make. The different-coloured patches are further embellished with applied braids and ribbons.

Patching route A: fabric bits are applied to the vilene and fabric jacket shapes and their edges covered with applied braid. It is easiest to apply all bits before putting on any braid.

symmetry so that one sleeve, for instance, is a mirror image of the other.

When you are happy with the placement of your pinned bits tack them in place and stitch, about 0.5cm in around the edge of each bit. I used small stab running stitches: you may prefer to use a machine. These stitches, worked right through to the lining of the jacket, will provide a soft quilted effect.

When all the applied bits are stitched in place, lay ribbon and braid lengths to cover the raw edges of the bits. Again, remember to make one front shape a mirror image of the other.

If you want to work more surface stitchery, say a monogram similar to that shown on my tennis dress (p 83), now is the time to do it. Make sure that none of the embroidery thread shows on the lining side.

Now you are ready to progress to final making-up instructions, which follow Patching route B.

Patching route B: paper
templates are covered with
fabric bits. Surplus fabric is
held over and tacked in
place. Neighbouring patches
are sewn together.

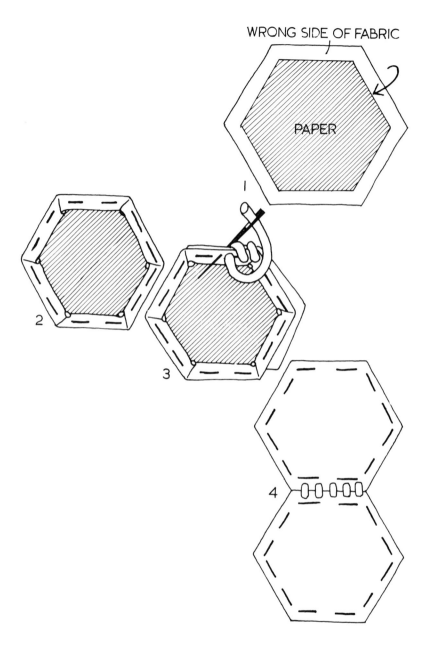

WRONG SIDE OF FABRIC

PAPER

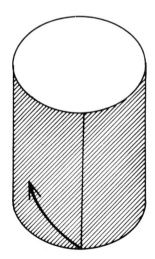

To make bias binding for the
jacket edges: sew 50cm fabric
into a tube and start cutting
diagonally. A second cut 2cm
away and parallel to the first
cut will produce bias binding
of that width.

Patching route B

This is the more conventional stitching method. It takes longer to do but can produce more exactly proportioned patches. For this method you will also need paper shapes the same as the lining and vilene joined shapes.

With a pencil divide the paper shapes into small hexagons, squares or whatever. Mark the bits with numbers so that you know how to fit them together again, and cut them out. Now form fabric patches around each paper bit and join neighbouring patches together along adjacent edges.

When an entire patchwork jacket shape has thus been completed, remove the paper bits and lay the patchwork on the vilene. Pin, tack around the edge of the shape, and work tiny running stitches or machine stitches around the edge of each patch. These stitches go right through to the lining and form light quilting.

You can then apply braids and ribbons as required and, as in route A, carefully work surface stitchery. Now you are ready for the final making-up.

Final making-up, for routes A and B

Sew the main seams of the jacket, with the shapes right sides together ('patches, braids and ribbons'). Press the seams open, cut to about 0.7cm from the stitching line and cover each pressed seam with a length of the satin ribbon. Stitch along each side of the ribbon. Sew the extra 50cm 'main' fabric into a tube and cut bias binding 3cm wide. Bind around neck, front and hem edges of the jacket and around both sleeves.

Your jacket is now finished. You will see that it is reversible. Worn 'lining side out' you have a smart one-fabric jacket with attractive ribbon binding. Worn 'right side out' you have a brightly-coloured different-fabric jacket that looks as if it has been made in Paris just for you!

Other ideas relating to these patchwork instructions

Why not make some of the patches from surplus fabric of skirts, dresses and trousers already in your wardrobe? Your jacket would then team up with many different outfits.

The same methods described here could also be used to make a lightly-quilted reversible wrap-around skirt.

24 Pulled thread tissue cover **

A friend of mine made tissue covers by the hundred, because her friends, like mine, appreciate pretty *and* useful things. I have copied her idea and I resolve to make lots of tissue covers for Christmas presents (they would also make nice 'hostess gifts' as thank-yous for hospitality).

The tissue cover illustrated is evenweave linen decorated with pulled thread. Because I made it for someone north of the border I have stitched it in green stranded cotton and lined it with heather-coloured fabric. At the end of this chapter I give alternative suggestions for embellishment.

To make this Scottish-inspired tissue cover you will need

An area of evenweave fabric 18.5 × 14cm (I used Glenshee evenweave, ivory, 132cm wide, 29 threads per 5cm)
A similar area of lining fabric (I used Jonelle heather-coloured batiste)
1 skein DMC stranded cotton (I used 906 green)
All-purpose thread to match your main fabric
Tacking cotton
Blunt and pointed needles (I used tapestry 24 and sharp 8)
Small pocket-size packet of tissues

A handy tissue cover would make a lovely present. This ivory linen cover is worked with bright green pulled thread and it is lined with heather-coloured fabric (case 8.3 × 11.6cm).

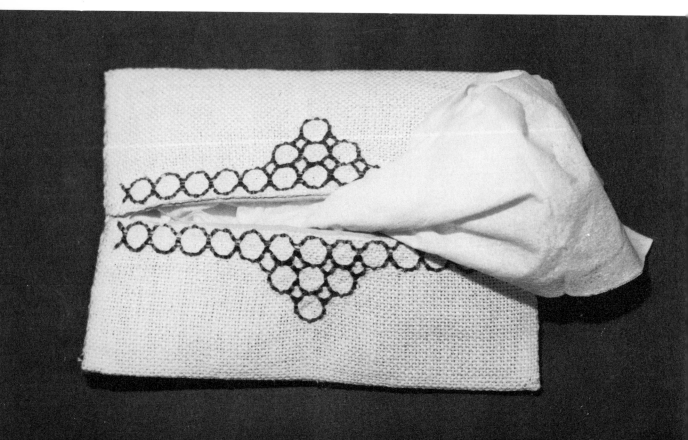

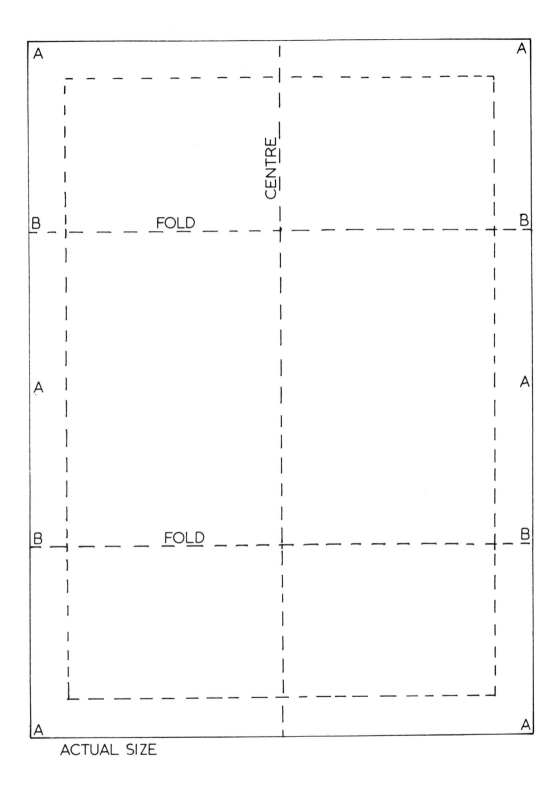

A   A

CENTRE

B   FOLD   B

A   A

B   FOLD   B

A   A

ACTUAL SIZE

Cut-out instructions for the
tissue case. Tackings should
be worked at all the dotted
lines.

Diagram of half of the pattern
Notice that the central
motifs, worked over 3 threads,
cannot exactly straddle the
central tacking line. The
base of the bottom motifs (c)
should be 3 threads up from
the end tackings. When all
the motifs have been worked
extra fillets (arrowed)
complete the pyramid effect.

The pattern is worked in
festoon stitch, a double back
stitch, over 3 threads (1).
Meandering half-circles (2)
are then infilled (dotted
stitches, 3): note that when a
second line of stitches works
over a previous line (black
stitches, 3) only 1 back stitch
is worked. (*For greater clarity,
these diagrams are not pulled.
As its name implies however
all pulled work should be
pulled tight.*)

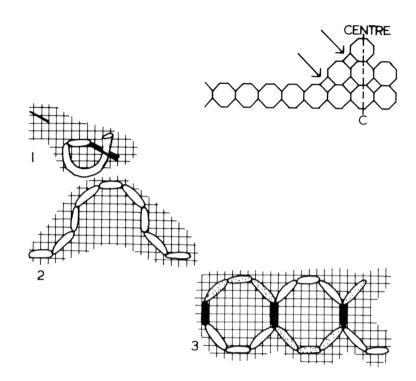

Tack your linen fabric with dividers as in the diagram here, and
oversew around all edges of the linen to prevent them fraying.
  I worked an identical pulled thread motif on what will be both ends
of the linen. Unlike drawn thread (in which threads are withdrawn)
in *pulled thread* fabric threads are simply pulled to produce a lacy
effect, and it is therefore a good idea to work with a short length of
embroidery thread that will be easier to pull *firmly*.
  Stitch with 2 strands of green on the tapestry needle. The design is
completely worked in pyramids of festoon stitch with each stitch
over 3 fabric threads. Follow the diagram and make sure that your
pattern is symmetrical both sides of the central tacking.
  When you have finished one end of the design, turn the fabric
through 180° and similarly embellish the other end.
  Press your work.

1 The finished linen piece is
laid on the backing, right
sides in, and stitched around
outer tackings with a 5cm
gap along one side. Surpluses
are trimmed and the
sandwich is turned right side
out.
2 After the gap has been
closed and the edges tacked
all around, the case is folded,
edges in to the centre and
linen side out, and all side
seams joined with oversewing.

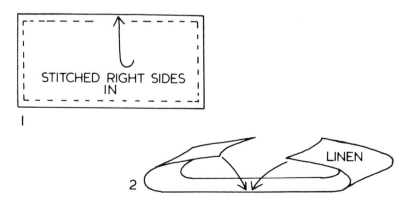

To make up the tissue case

Lay the lining and linen together right sides in, and stitch around all the 'outer seam' lines, leaving a 5cm gap. Trim the surplus fabric, especially at the corners of the piece, and then turn it right side out through the 5cm gap. Tack around the edges of the piece, tucking in the surplus around the gap and closing the hole with oversewing.

Following the 'fold' tackings on the linen, make two bends in the cover, linen side out, and oversew along the AB lines with small oversewing.

Other ideas for this project

Choose the colour combination (fabric, thread, lining) to suit your friend's wardrobe.

Instead of pulled thread use blackwork or cross stitch to embellish the cover.

Dispense with lining fabric. Make neat mitres at the corner surpluses of the linen to give a self-facing.

By measuring the required size and adding 1cm all around, for seam surplus, make a similar cover for a square or larger rectangular packet of tissues.

By doubling the size given here, and lining the case with washable plastic, make a small make-up case. Sew in a zip fastener before you stitch the sides together.

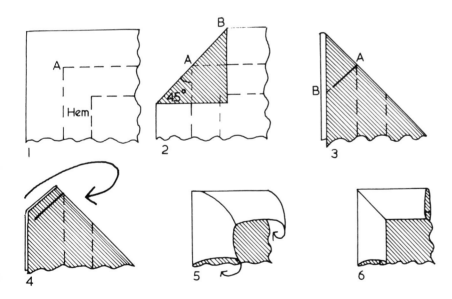

To mitre a corner of a hem:
1 Excess fabric, the same width as the desired hem plus 8mm, is left outside what will eventually be the edge of the item (A marking the desired corner point.)
2 To guide subsequent sewing, a crease is made across that corner, passing through A at 45°. 3 Working from the wrong side of the fabric, (shaded here) a neat seam is sewn, by hand or machine, from A to within 8mm of B. 4 Excess corner fabric is cut away and the sewn corner is turned inside out. 5 The outer 8mm is turned under. 6 This produces a neat, mitred, corner.

25 Quilt your camera case*

My Minolta 450E is indispensable. It has its own carrying cord, which sensibly doubles as a measure to gauge the distance for close-up shots. But I needed a case for it that would give protection and be so bright and colourful that I would not leave it behind somewhere.

I therefore made this quilted case. The measurements will fit any 110 size camera, and can be adapted to fit other sizes.

The case is machine washable and therefore practical. The outside is drip-dry striped seersucker and its padding is foam rubber. It is lined completely with white cotton lawn, and it fastens with velcro.

Quilting, as you can read fully in *The Coats Book of Embroidery* (p 214ff), consists generally of stitching together 2 or more layers of material with padding. Traditionally quilting stitches were often small stab running stitches: I worked this case on a Frister + Rossmann Cub 4 sewing machine with no special equipment but you might prefer to quilt your case by hand.

A practical washable quilted case which fits any 110 camera: this one was machine-quilted but you may prefer to stitch by hand.

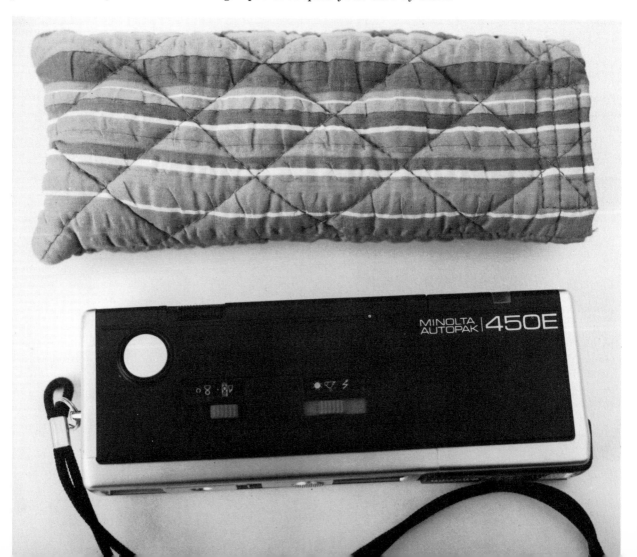

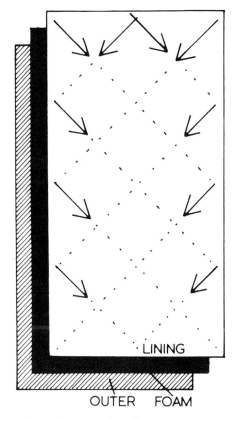

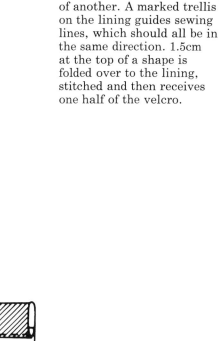

Lining, foam and outer shapes, here shown in order, are placed directly one on top of another. A marked trellis on the lining guides sewing lines, which should all be in the same direction. 1.5cm at the top of a shape is folded over to the lining, stitched and then receives one half of the velcro.

To make a quilted camera case you will need

2 areas of outer fabric, each piece 7cm taller than the length of your camera and 7cm wider than its width (I used a Jonelle seersucker)

2 areas of white cotton lawn (I used McLawn) the same size as the outer fabrics

2 pieces of thin foam rubber each the size of the fabrics

All-purpose thread, white, and also the colour in which you want to 'quilt'

Pointed needle for hand-sewing (I used a sharp 8). If you are going to quilt by hand you will also need a longer needle, say a crewel 10

4cm velcro 1.5cm wide

'Invisible' marker

With the 'invisible' pen (its marks will vanish when you first wash your case) mark a trellis over the white lawn pieces. My trellis had lines 3.5cm from each other.

Form a sandwich of outer fabric, foam centrally placed and the white lawn above it. Pin and tack. Working from the markings on the lawn side, stitch along all the marked lines, always starting lines in the same direction.

Fold 1.5cm at the top of 1 shape over to the lining. Turn the surplus under, pin and stitch down. Place 1 of the velcro halves centrally, parallel with the edge of the shape. Do the same with the other shape.

Place both shapes together, right sides in, and pin down both sides and across the base so that there is about 1.75cm surplus in

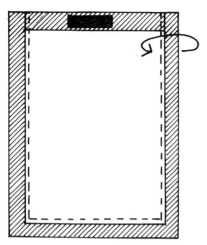

The 2 shapes are placed right sides together and stitched down both sides and across the base. One surplus is cut close to the stitching line and the other is folded over to the lining of the other shape and hemmed.

If you prefer another quilting technique you might like to decorate your camera case shapes with Italian quilting. In this instance you stitch through main outer fabric (white here) and lining (checked here) in parallel lines, and thick thread padding is then taken through the channels from the lining side (2).

each direction if you lay the camera on the shapes. Try the camera inside to see if it is a good 'fit' and, if necessary, adjust accordingly.

Stitch around the sides and base of the case. Cut the surplus from one side of each seam right back almost to the stitching line. Trim the other seam side to 1.5cm.

This is where I started hand-sewing as I did not want my seam-finishing to show on the right side of the case. Unless you want to bind your seam in another way I suggest you too thread up a short length of white thread. Turn the surplus 1.5cm of each seam side over the cut side and hem it to the white lining without going through to the main fabric.

Turn the case inside out . . . and you have finished!

Other ideas relating to this project

Quilt a larger bag for a larger camera, or a smaller bag for a smaller camera.

Make your case in brocade or a similar lush fabric and add a ribbon handle for a little Victorian-style evening reticule.

Fit the case to accommodate eyeglasses or sunglasses.

Add a pocket to one of the quilted shapes – before you join them together – to hold film.

Use the same measurements of outer and lining fabrics and discard the foam shapes. Quilt the fabrics in 'Italian quilting' with pairs of lines of little stab stitches forming a required pattern. Working from the lining you then thread thick washable white yarn through the prepared channels.

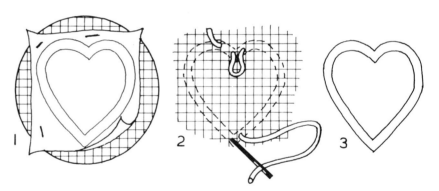

26 Raisedwork miniature ***

I have long been fascinated by raisedwork, the three-dimensional technique that was especially popular in the 17th century (today it is generally known as stumpwork, and there is now a Stumpwork Society for all devotees both to the collecting and the working of this embroidery).

My little king is 12cm tall (with his crown on). He stands by himself, and he holds in one hand a long sceptre with jewelled top. He wears a short blue striped robe and, over it, a marvellous full red cloak, edged with ermine and lined with blue and gold Damascus brocade and with an ermine collar. His crown is also jewelled. He has green stockings and brown shoes.

If you have even reasonably deft fingers you will have fun working a little king like this. As well as the materials listed below you will need patience, a basic knowledge of needlepoint, and good enough eyesight to work on 22 canvas. Have fun!

To make the little king you will need

Area of 22 mono canvas (110 holes per 5cm), 20 × 30cm
Area of rich brocade, or similar lining fabric, 12 × 20cm
Area of vilene soft iron-on interfacing 20 × 30cm
Area of vilene bondaweb 20 × 20cm

Threads
DMC stranded cottons, 1 skein each 350, 498, 902 (3 reds for the cloak), 2 skeins white (for the ermine), 1 skein 543 (for hands and arms)
DMC coton-à-broder, 1 skein 938 brown (for ermine 'tails' and shoes), 1 skein each 800, 799 and 797 (3 blues for the robe)
DMC gold embroidery thread, 1 reel (crown and shoe laces)
Elsa Williams cloisonne (sceptre shaft)
All-purpose sewing threads to match darkest blue, darkest red, white and brown embroidery threads
Tacking thread

Needles
Tapestry 22, small and large pointed (I used crewel 10 and 4) and beading needle

Assorted beads
Old-fashioned wooden clothes peg 11cm high
Pipe cleaner
14cm length florist's wire
Small amount of doll's hair
Flesh-coloured acrylic paint and brush
Wide felt marker, dark green, for painting his stockings
Black NEPO marker
Copydex adhesive
Masking tape, narrow, about 10cm long
Blu-tack, or similar – a small amount to make him stand

opposite Miniature king, 12cm tall, holds a regal sceptre. He wears a rich 'ermine'-trimmed and brocade-lined cloak.

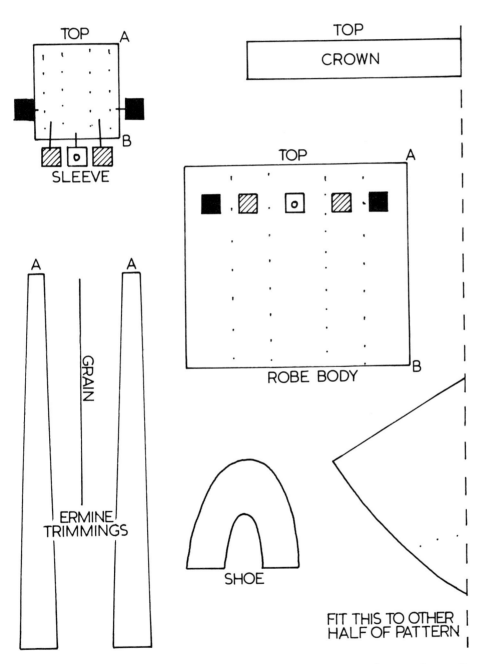

TOP

CROWN

TOP A

SLEEVE

B

TOP A

ROBE BODY

B

A A

GRAIN

ERMINE TRIMMINGS

SHOE

FIT THIS TO OTHER HALF OF PATTERN

First lay the canvas above the cut-out instructions diagram here and NEPO-mark outlines for 2 sleeves, 1 robe body, 2 cloak facings, 1 cloak, 1 collar, 2 shoes and 1 crown. I suggest you stitch all the canvas areas before you cut these pieces.

Cut-out instructions for shapes on 22 canvas.

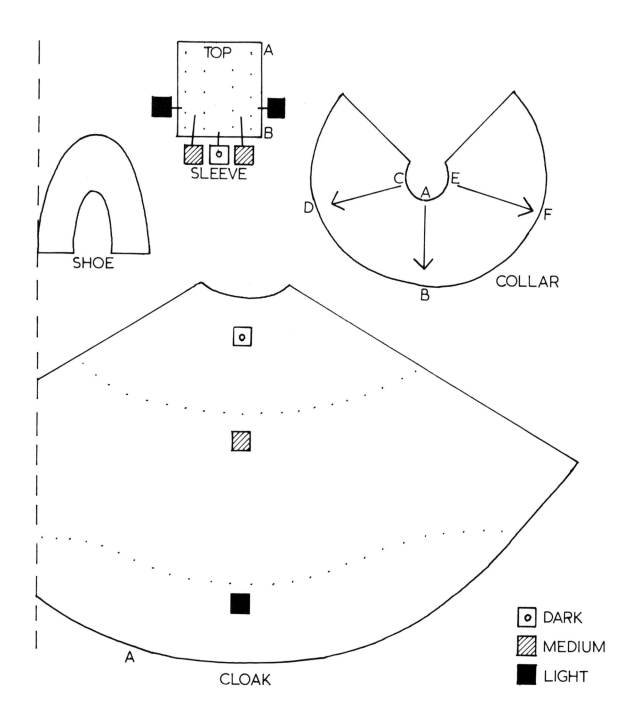

TOP

A

B

SLEEVE

SHOE

C A E

D

F

B

COLLAR

DARK

MEDIUM

LIGHT

A

CLOAK

122

Robe body

Working from top to bottom and starting at A, work rows of tyler rose stitch as illustrated. Start with dark blue, progress to medium blue and to light blue and then to medium and dark blue. You can then, if you like, chainstitch a necklace and add a bead as pendant.

Robe sleeves

Similar blue stripes as indicated. Again, start stitching at A and work from top to bottom of each sleeve.

Cloak body

Work rows of bargello with all 6 strands (stripped and put back together) of red stranded cottons. Start at A and work across in the formation indicated. Shade from darkest red, the shade you start with, through medium to lightest red.

Cloak trimmings

White stranded cottons, all 6 strands, split stitches over 5, 6 or 7 threads as you like, to give a staggered effect. Start at the top of each trimming (A) and work to the base. Ermine 'tails' are then worked, in brown straight stitches in V shapes.

Collar

Split stitch, white, all 6 strands of white stranded cotton. Start at A and work stitches until you reach the circumference at B. Then start at C and work to D and E to F and thereafter similar radial lines, working enough main 'stakes' for you subsequently to be able easily and with equal density to fill the whole area. Work ermine 'tails'.

Shoes

Dark brown tent stitch.

Crown

DMC gold, satin stitches from top to bottom, vertically, between each warp thread.

When you have finished all the canvas stitching, iron vilene soft iron-on interfacing on to the back of the canvas. With the exception of the crown (leave this), cut the worked motifs out leaving 5mm surplus all around. Turn the surpluses under and tack around the edges of all motifs before binding, with buttonhole stitch in an appropriate all-purpose sewing thread, the hem lines of the robe body and 2 sleeves, cloak body, ermine trimmings and collar. Similarly buttonhole-bind the 2 sides of the cloak, the 2 long sides of each of the trimmings and the neck of the collar.

At this stage you can turn to the figure itself. Paint the head of the clothes peg with flesh-coloured paint and felt-pen the two 'legs' in dark green pen. Place the clothes peg under the pipe cleaner as illustrated and bind the cleaner in place with masking tape. Wrap both 'hands' and 'arms' with 6 strands of flesh-coloured stranded

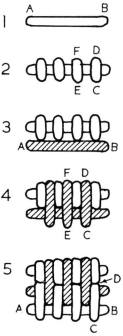

When working tyler rose stitch you will find it easier to turn the canvas through 90° so that AB is horizontal. Tyler rose is a form of self couching. First make a long stitch AB (1) and, on the return, couch, over the canvas threads either side of the AB stitch and into every other available space (2). Your next line of stitching (shaded here) starts with another long line AB one canvas thread below the first AB (3). When you return, you couch over the first and second long AB stitches, in the interstices of the first couchings, and over 3 canvas threads (4). Thereafter, however, on the return journey you couch over the last 2 AB long stitches to meet couchings of 2 rows before, but you only couch over 2 canvas threads, those immediately below and immediately above the last AB stitch (5). When you reach the dotted markings on your canvas start stitching with another shade of thread. This will give a zigzag colour change.

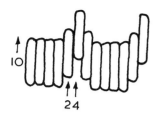

Cloak bargello pattern. All stitches are worked over 10 canvas threads and the steps are 2 and 4 threads high. When you reach dotted markings on your canvas start stitching with another shade of thread.

cotton. When the flesh 'face' has dried NEPO mark facial features (on an area of head above 'leg' separation).

To *dress him in his robe* you can now, with blue all-purpose thread, sew together the side seams of each sleeve (turning the surpluses under). Fit a sleeve over an 'arm' and stitch the shoulder surplus to the pipe cleaner. Fix the other sleeve in the same way. Join the central back seam of the robe body and fix it in place (you may have to make 2 vertical cuts to accommodate the arms: these will not cause fraying as the canvas is backed with interfacing). The hem of the robe should rest about 3.5cm from the bottom of the peg. Do not worry if the tops of the robe and sleeves look messy: they will be covered by the cloak.

Now *form and fit the cloak*. Cut appropriate small areas of bondaweb and seal the 2 ermine trimmings to either side of the cloak. Cut appropriate shapes of brocade and bondaweb and seal the brocade as lining to the cloak. Use big stitches (which will not later show) to attach the top of the cloak to the figure: the back of the cloak should rest lightly on the ground. Do not worry if the top of the cloak looks messy: this will be covered by the collar.

The *collar* will 'neaten' the appearance of the robe and cloak. Making sure that the neck opening will just fit over the head, carefully sew, with white all-purpose thread, the back seam of the collar, surplus canvases turned under. Fit the collar in place.

His *hair* needs attention next. Only a small amount is required. Sew the hair with dark brown all-purpose thread, and when the 'wig' is formed, glue it to the top of the head. Do not at this stage trim his hair.

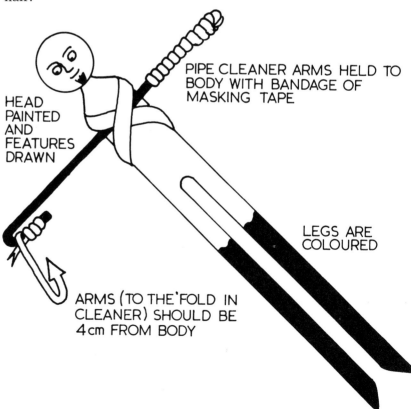

HEAD PAINTED AND FEATURES DRAWN

PIPE CLEANER ARMS HELD TO BODY WITH BANDAGE OF MASKING TAPE

LEGS ARE COLOURED

ARMS (TO THE 'FOLD IN CLEANER) SHOULD BE 4cm FROM BODY

After the pipe cleaner is attached with masking tape, start binding each end with stranded cotton. When you are about 3.7cm from the body double back the pipe cleaner and bind over the 2 thicknesses of cleaner. Bind almost to the shoulders and secure the thread end with a small bit of masking tape.

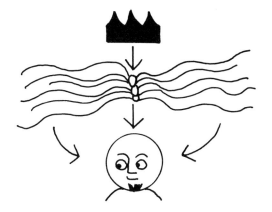

Work a few brown back stitches binding the middle of your length of hair. Apply a small amount of copydex to fix this stitching to the top of the head. The flowing ends of the hair will be subsequently brought to the sides and back of the head when the crown is put on.

To make the king stand securely *shoes* are required. Cut away all surplus canvas from curved lines and oversew the stitched edges (if stubbly bits of canvas show, disguise them with NEPO). Stitch together back seams to form 2 shoes, and if you want shoelaces work little bows with gold thread and, perhaps, a bead. Fit a shoe over a 'foot' and stuff the space underneath the shoe with a small lump of Blu-tack. Fit the other shoe in the same manner.

A king needs the trappings of regality! To make his *sceptre*, fold the wire in 2 and wrap the entire thing with gold cloissonne thread: you can hold the thread ends with a small bit of masking tape wrapped around the 2 wire ends. Into this masking tape carefully stitch as many beads as you like.

Now return to the *crown* shape you have stitched. Cut a 5mm surplus to the base of the crown, turn it under and hold in place with DMC gold buttonhole stitch. Now very carefully cut the top of your crown to the shape you want (a zigzag or whatever), making sure you do not snip through your earlier satin stitching. Attach beads as you think fit. Cut to a 5mm surplus either side of the crown, and join these 2 edges to form the crown's seam, the surpluses turned under (you will find that you can manage this rather tricky little seam easier if you fit the crown over one of your fingers). If you want to cover up this seam you can stitch on more beads.

Fit the crown in place and trim the king's hair if you think it is too long. If he still is not regal enough for your liking stitch on bead finger rings, make leg garters, put beads on his cloak. I do hope you enjoyed making him (and I should love to see a photograph of *your* finished sovereign!).

Other ideas for making raisedwork miniatures

Why not design and make a queen to accompany the king?
Using the above formula you could design an entire gallery of, say, American presidents, or famous women of the past.
A school class could compile an entire nativity set using this formula.

27 Sample 'family tree' **

So many people have asked me how to make a family tree as a result of the picture on p 107 of *The Coats Book of Embroidery* that I have reworked the picture, and here it is.

This is my family tree, with my sisters' names, my parents' names and the 2 family names. It is, admittedly, a simplified genealogical tree, but I have found that when people understand the recipe for a tree with only 3 'levels' they can then progress to more complicated versions!

My tree is worked on Glenshee evenweave with DMC stranded cottons. I have used only cross stitch.

To make your family tree you will need

> Area of linen 40 × 30cm (I used Glenshee evenweave with 60 threads per 5cm)
> 7 skeins of DMC stranded cottons, 606 red, 938 dark brown, 434 medium brown, 437 lightest brown, 895 dark green, 906 medium green, 3348 lightest green
> Tacking cotton
> Blunt needle (I used tapestry 24)
> Calculator, ruler, graph paper and pencils

First you should jot down the names you want to stitch. I suggest that, unlike my prototype, you do not work a Christian and surname together. Draw in hyphens from one name to another. Then, using the alphabet on p 89, write out each name. Calculate how many squares across each name uses. Take your *longest* name and find the halfway point across. Using this halfway point as your centre, design a symmetrical 'fruit' around it.

Draw out on your graph paper enough similarly sized and shaped fruits to accommodate the other names. Find the halfway point across on each name and 'centre' the name, writing it in a fruit shape.

Now plan how many squares you want for your hyphens (I suggest a maximum of 13 squares). You can have straight vertical, horizontal or diagonal hyphens or 'trailing branches'.

Take another sheet of graph paper and draw out an appropriate number of appropriately placed fruits separated by the right length and shape of hyphens (there is no need to write out the names within the fruits).

Count how many squares across your design occupies. Count how many squares up and down your design occupies. Find the *centre* of your entire design. *Note:* if you have occupied *more than 120 squares across* you should shorten your hyphens.

It is now time to stitch! First run tackings dividing your fabric, held portraitwise (long sides up), into quadrants.

You have your centre point of fabric. You know the centre point of your design . . . so stitch from the centre out. Since you are going

opposite A project for you to design *yourself!* Plan and work your *own* family tree – this chapter tells you how to set about it. (Project is for a tree worked with one name per 'fruit', the whole thing worked in 2 strands of DMC stranded cotton over 2 threads of evenweave linen.)

COBBAN
MARLOW
JAMES
LORNA
MARY
GOSTELOW
DIANA
MAY
HILARY
WHARTON
HELENA
RACHED

After you have jotted down the names and their connecting hyphens (1), you should write out all those names on graph paper and find the halfway points across (2). The longest name is then written out again and centred and a symmetrical fruit planned around it (3).

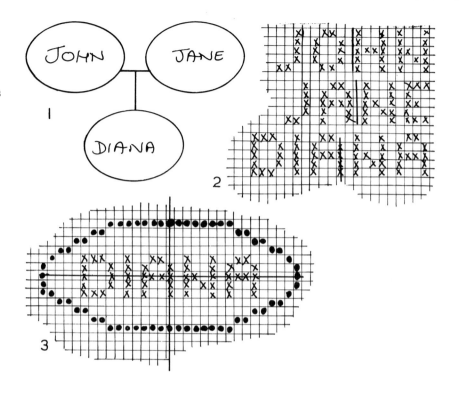

to stitch entirely in *2 strands*, cross stitch over *2 linen threads*, you may have to begin your central stitch by straddling 1 thread each side of your vertical tackings.

You should have all the fruits (stitched in red) and hyphens (stitched in medium brown) finished before tacking an outline around all the group. Similarly tack in a trunk outline.

You can infill the trunk in 3 browns, vertical rows darkest to one side, medium in the middle, and lightest to the other side.

I then worked several basic leaf motifs in darkest green. I variously turned my fabric through 90° or 180° or 270° to produce different looking leaves all in fact copied from the same asymmetrical motif. Note that no leaves extend outside the tree outline tackings and none protrude on top of a hyphen, though leaves can continue uninterrupted, as it were, the other side. No leaves should be worked on top of the outline of a fruit or continue into it.

I spotted my leaves variously to cover uneven parts of the available linen. Then I worked more and more leaves, always sticking to the basic motif. First I worked in medium green and then lightest green.

When I thought I had done enough leaves – I meant the foliage to be uneven to make it look more natural – I removed all my tackings and my sampler was ready!

Other ideas relating to this project

Use your finished tree to embellish the cover of a family photograph album.

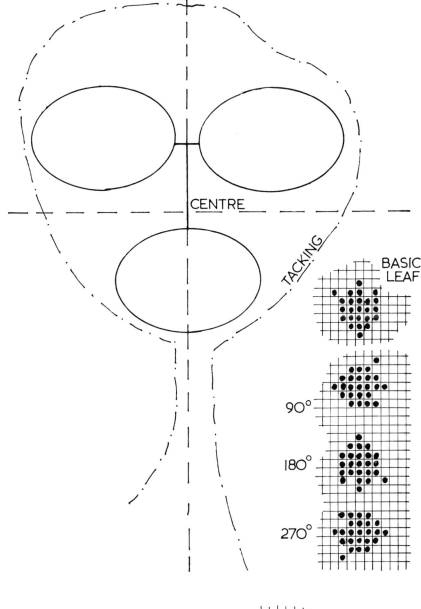

After you have stitched all the fruits and hyphens on your linen, tack the outline of a tree encompassing at least part of all the fruits. The main part of the tree can then be filled with basic leaf motifs variously upright or turned through 90°, 180° or 270°.

CENTRE

TACKING

BASIC LEAF

90°

180°

270°

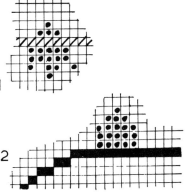

Leaves can be bisected by hyphens and continue unperturbed the other side (1). Leaves must stop at fruits (2).

28 Shadow-work pincushion ✳✳✳

As a change from purely practical projects I had the greatest fun designing and making an utterly feminine pincushion. The front has white organdie backed with pale blue satin to show the organdie's stitching. A white rose design is worked in running and satin stitches: part of the flower is worked through 2 layers of organdie to give more of a shadow effect.

The cushion cover has a backing of white satin and peripheral piping. Inside is a small pillow pad.

To work the rose embroidery you will need

> White organdie 20 × 20cm
> Small piece of organdie, about 6 × 6cm
> 1 skein DMC stranded cotton white
> Pointed needle (I used sharp 8 but crewel 8 could suffice)
> Pale blue all-purpose thread
> Rustless pins
> Frame (I used my 10cm hoop)
> Invisible marker

Choose in which direction you want your rose to face (turn the design through 90° if you prefer) and lay your organdie accordingly above the rose design. Mark the outline of all areas of the rose, stem and leaves on the fabric with invisible marker (if you do not want to disfigure the page of the book you could trace the design on to plain paper before transferring it to the fabric).

Place the smaller organdie underneath the main organdie, warp threads at 45° to those of the main organdie, so that the application completely covers the shaded part of the design. Pin in place and tack with all-purpose thread (pale blue, so that if a small part of the tacking thread cannot later be removed it will hardly show).

Now all your stitching will be with white stranded cotton. Remember that all stitches show in shadow-work so do not begin or finish threads with a mess: begin with 1 or 2 little back stitches on the line along which you are shortly going to work and finish in the same way. Similarly, do not take your thread from one area of the motif to another. Stop and start again.

Put the organdies in the frame and work minute running stitches, through both layers, around all the marked lines of the rose flower in 1 strand. Take the organdies out of the frame and, working from the reverse of the work, carefully cut away the surplus application, that is to say all the smaller organdie outside the shaded area and in the section marked X. Put the organdie back in the frame.

All the edges of the rose area will be worked in close satin stitch with 3 strands of thread. Think of the rose as an odd-shaped wheel, and make an invisible marker dot in the centre of the rose (the section marked X). Work your satin stitches all aiming in to the dot. As with the broderie anglaise housecoat (p 31), if you want to pad

opposite Shadow-work shows to most effect when it has a coloured backing. This pincushion, 15cm square, has a front panel of organdie which is backed with blue satin: the cushion is edged with satin piping and the reverse is white satin.

Rose design. You can set it as you want on your fabric but when you apply the smaller bit of organdie it should be at 45° to the grain of the main fabric.

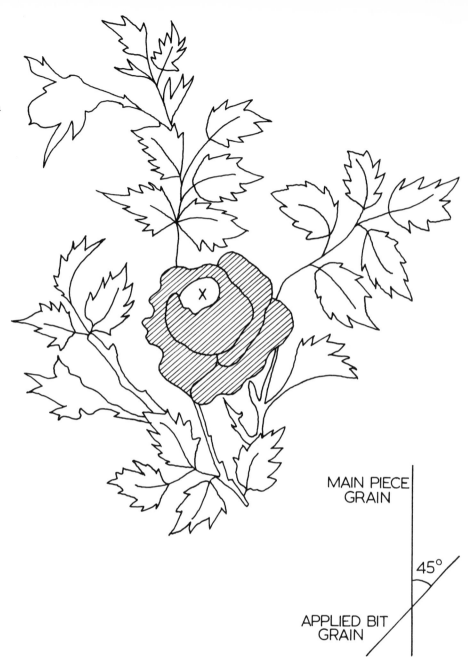

MAIN PIECE GRAIN

45°

APPLIED BIT GRAIN

some of the areas to be worked in satin stitch you can make back, running or other stitches before you do the satin stitch.

You can see from the photograph and from the diagram how I worked little running stitches on the petals to give extra shading. All these lines of stitches should be parallel to each other.

The rose really is the hardest part of this design! You now have the simpler stem and leaves to work. These are all 1 strand, little running stitches: when you place the organdie against a coloured fabric the lines of stitches appear continuous. Notice that the rose leaves are pointed and try to achieve sharp angles by stopping and starting again as illustrated.

When you have finished all the stitching run the fabric under a cold tap (not warm or hot) and the blue lines will disappear.

To make your little rose into a pincushion you will need

A finished rose panel (as above)
Coloured satin (I used pale blue) 17 × 17cm
White satin 17 × 17cm
Bias tape made with satin cut on bias folded over and
machined around with piping cord, length of bias at least
60cm
White all-purpose sewing thread
Small cushion pad with rounded corners, measurements
14 × 14cm

Tack the embroidery right side up to the right side of the coloured
satin. Lay the piping bias around the edge of the organdie, rounding
the corners as illustrated. Tack and machine stitch as close as
possible to the piping cord, 1cm in from the edges of the organdie and
satin.

Place the white satin face downwards on to the organdie and tack
around the edges. Machine stitch on top of the previous machining,
leaving 9cm open along one side. Trim surplus fabrics, and turn the
cushion cover right side out. Insert your cushion pad, and stitch the
hole together with neat hemming. Your pretty pincushion is finished
(the only trouble is, it is too dainty to hold mere pins!).

Other ideas for your shadow-work design

Fill your cushion pad not with ordinary padding but with lavender,
herbs or pot pourri.
Instead of working with white stranded cotton try stitching with a
pale pink or blue thread.
Use a finished rose design to make an extra pocket panel for a white
silk shirt.
Insert the finished rose on to a larger wedding or christening cushion.
Work several similar rose panels, half of them reversed as mirror
images, to be applied down the sides of a wedding veil.

A small invisible marker dot
in the centre of the rose
helps you to direct all your
stitches towards the 'hub' of
the 'wheel'. Close satin
stitches (black area) bind the
edges of the rose and the
centre. Neat lines of running
stitches add further shading.

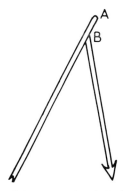

To achieve exact points for
the rose's leaves and thorns,
exaggerate the points as
indicated.

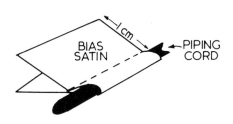

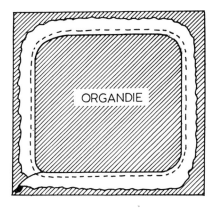

Satin-covered piping cord is
required for the edging of the
cushion. At least 60cm of
piping is required, with
surplus fabric at least 1cm
deep.

After the organdie is tacked,
right side up, to the right
side of the coloured satin, the
piping is laid, cord side in,
around the edges of the
fabrics, corners rounded.
Machine stitching is worked
around, 1cm from fabric
edges, as close to the cord as
possible.

133

29 Smock a family heirloom **

Many families already have treasured christening robes, worn by generation after generation of babies. In the past such robes were often exquisitely tucked, embroidered and embellished with lace, all of which must have taken ages to do.

But in this day of practicality and shortage of time, you may like to think about making a christening cape like this. It can be worn over the baby's everyday clothes and it fits any size of small child as elasticity is provided by a smocked band. It is machine-washable and drip-dry.

I made my cape in lightweight white batiste, and I stitched it partly in pale yellow so that the decoration would show up in the photograph. As you can see, the cape falls from a smocked band, above which there is a soft neck ruff. Two ribbons are attached to the smocking so that the cape can be tied on the baby. The side and hem seams are turned outwards, to the right side of the garment, to avoid any possible roughness upsetting the wearer. I stitched my seams on a Frister + Rossmann Cub 4 but you could hand-stitch, with hemming or another technique.

The baby's christening cape measures 73cm from the smocking. (It is machine-washable and drip-dry.)

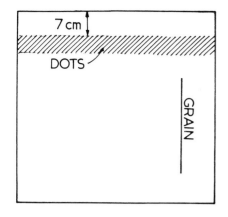

Smocking dots are placed across the top of the fabric (smocking area shaded). Five rows 1cm apart of dots 6mm from each other are required.

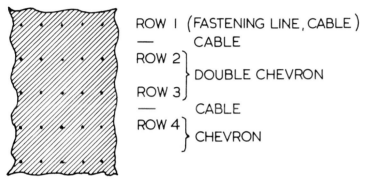

ROW 1 (FASTENING LINE, CABLE)
— CABLE
ROW 2 ⎫
⎬ DOUBLE CHEVRON
ROW 3 ⎭
— CABLE
ROW 4 ⎫
⎬ CHEVRON

To make a baby's christening cape you will need

90cm white batiste at least 100cm wide (I used a Jonelle batiste 114cm wide)
1m white satin ribbon 1.5cm wide
1 skein DMC stranded cotton white
White all-purpose thread
Pointed needle (I used crewel 8)
Smocking dots (enough to give you 5 rows of dots 6mm apart right across 100cm of fabric, rows 1cm beneath each other).
If you do not have any smocking dots, you will need an 'invisible' pen and a ruler

Place your smocking dots, ink side down, across the fabric so that the top row is 7cm beneath the top of the fabric. Tack in place and press so that the dots are transferred. Remove the tackings and the paper. If you are measuring dots, go ahead and similarly make your top row 7cm from the top of the fabric.

Using a length of white all-purpose thread at least 50cm long, work long tacking stitches from one end of a row to the other, making sure you start each line with a secure knot. Leave the other end of thread loose but when you have worked another line tie both loose ends so that the threads do not slip back along the rows.

When you have worked all 5 lines of tackings, gather them *as tight as you can*, 'stroking' the pleats with your needle to make sure they fall correctly. Secure the white thread ends with knots.

Smocking consists of horizontal rows of stitches worked on the tip of each of the folds. Thread up a length of stranded cotton (3 strands)

To prepare the smocking area, make tiny stitches at each dot. When the first line of tackings (1) is completed, a parallel line at row two is worked (2). When all the lines are worked (3) loose ends are pulled as tight as possible and tied.

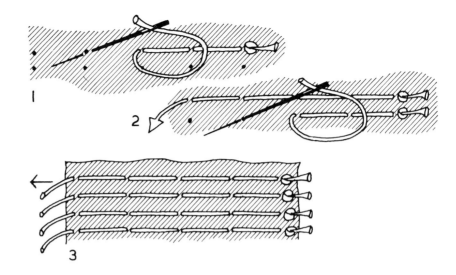

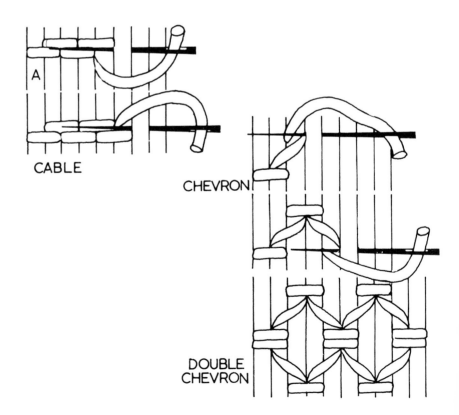

CABLE

CHEVRON

DOUBLE CHEVRON

Cable and chevron smocking techniques are used: each vertical section (A) shown here represents the pleat formed by the tackings.

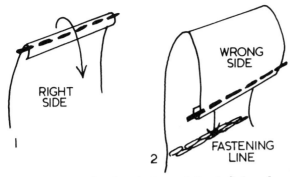

RIGHT SIDE

WRONG SIDE

1

2

FASTENING LINE

After side and hem seams have been secured, the top surplus, above the smocking, is turned over to the right side and gathering worked (1). The surplus is then turned over, gatherings pulled to fit the fastening smocking line when stretched to the maximum, and hemmed neatly on to that fastening line (2).

and make a few minute back stitches at the left-hand end of the top row. Following the guideline of the smocking dots, work a 'fastening line' of cable stitch across to the right-hand end of the row. Finish the line with a few small back stitches at the right-hand dot. Work a similar line of rope stitches parallel to this fastening line, halfway between the first and second rows of dots.

Next I suggest you progress to a double line of chevron stitch. The first line is worked between the second dot and halfway down to the third dot, and the second line works between that halfway point and the third dot. Another line of cable stitch (halfway down to the fourth dot) is then produced above a single chevron (fourth dot and halfway down to the fifth dot).

When you have finished all the stitching, carefully remove the white tackings and wash the fabric so that the transfer dots disappear.

To make up the cape you should first turn a main hem, 1.5cm deep, up to the right side of the smocking. Tack. Then form side hems by turning a small amount of fabric outside the outer dots back to the right side of the smocking. Tack, and stitch around all 3 turned back hems.

Even if you have so far hem-stitched by machine you will have to form the ruff by hand. Make a small hem, 5mm deep, the fabric turned over to the right side of the smocking, with gathering stitches. Gather this hem so that it fits the fastening smocking line when it is extended to *maximum* elasticity. Pin this hem over to the fastening line (right side of fabric) and neatly hem it, catching the hem to each of the cable stitches of the fastening line. Leave the ends of the ruff open.

Cut the ribbon in half and sew one end of one piece to the narrow seam at one end of the smocking and similarly attach the other piece of ribbon.

Other ideas for this smocking project

Work a similar cape in velvet for a Christmas garment.

Adapt the pattern, giving twice the width of smocking on a larger area of fabric, the length from the wearer's shoulders to the ground plus 7cm, to form an older child's cape.

Instead of forming the smocked panel into a baby's christening cape, make it into a lady's apron. Hem around both sides and the hem of a finished smocking, cut the surplus off close above the fastening line and stitch bias binding over this cut, the binding stitched to the fastening line. Add side ties and you have a lovely Christmas present for an adult!

30 White wedding dress **

Most wedding dresses as such are worn only once (well, seriously, how many people do in fact wear the dress again to the many parties that they envisage it being 'just right for'?).

This, however, *is* a dress that can be used and used. Without its sleeved jacket it makes a versatile sun or evening dress with its delicate shoestring straps. It can be chopped short and/or easily dyed.

Its main claim to fame, however, is its economy! I made the full-length dress and jacket in a Very Easy Vogue Pattern in white batiste, lined the dress and trimmed all outer edges with English Sewing Cotton's F24 trimming, embroidered the back of the jacket with a single skein of DMC's stranded cotton – and came out with change from £10!

To make the white wedding dress you will need

A simple dress and jacket pattern
Ample lightweight white fabric (I required 3.60m of 112cm wide Jonelle batiste)
Lining for the dress (I bought 1.80m of Jonelle lining)
Enough lace trimming to decorate all edges (I made my garment first and then measured that I should need 5.50m of F24 trimming)
Required notions (for this pattern, I needed a 40cm zip fastener, I dispensed with interfacing)
White all-purpose thread
1 skein DMC stranded cotton white (I cheated! To make the stitching show better in the photograph I stitched with pale geranium thread)
'Invisible' pen
Frame (I used my 10cm hoop)

First make up the dress and jacket according to the pattern instructions. I found my chosen pattern very easy to follow, the written instructions were extremely clear. (You may prefer to cut out all your shapes and do the embroidery on the back jacket shape before making it up. I, however, wanted to see how the finished outfit would look!)

When I had both garments finished, I carefully stored the dress in a full-length plastic bag – washed my hands yet again, took a deep breath, and started embellishing the back of the jacket.

Using the invisible marker, note the centre line of the back of your jacket from neck to hem. Now lay the jacket over the appropriate area of the design set out here. (If the outline does not show through clearly enough, remove the fabric and go over the paper outline with black marker. Wait for it to dry and then replace the fabric.) Mark the outlines on the fabric with invisible pen.

Remove the fabric and place a part of the design in the frame. First stitch the *grapes:* outline them with tiny back stitches (2 strands)

It is the back of the bride that will be seen clearly as she walks down the aisle . . . a floral bouquet embellishes the back of the jacket. The shoestring strap petticoat dress can easily be adapted later or worn as an evening gown.

A

B

CENTRE

BASE OF JACKET

Design (grapes marked with 'x', central flower shaded).

CENTRE

141

Grapes are formed of padded satin stitch.
1 Outline each grape with small back stitches.
2 Partly infill with straight stitches.
3 Work closely parallel satin stitches over, and at right angles to, those straight stitches.

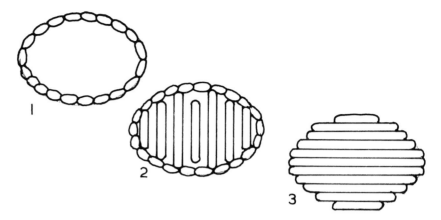

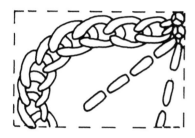

The central motif is formed thus: all the main outlines are chainstitch, petal shading is small running stitch and the centre is partly infilled with french knots.

and then work several interior straight stitches (3 strands) to provide padding for subsequent satin stitch (3 strands). Try to get the direction of stitches varying from grape to grape.

The main *central flower* is outlined with chainstitch (3 strands) and the centre partly filled with french knots (3 strands). Petal shading is lines of running stitch (1 strand). *All other outlines* are back stitch (2 strands).

When all the embroidery is finished, run cold water over the design and the blue lines will disappear! Now you have flowers on your back to complement the flowers you hold before you . . . and here is wishing you *all* happiness and love.

Other ideas from this project

Why make it in white? How about a black outfit stitched in gold? Make the dress short and you have a sun dress and an evening jacket that could make you the neatest cocktailer around.
You could stitch the embroidery in a variety of different coloured threads and make simple shoestring dresses in some of those colours. This would provide an extremely useful and varied holiday wardrobe.

Main stitches

As well as stitches already drawn for particular projects, these are some of the most popular embroidery stitches (a comprehensive selection of further stitches can be found in my embroidery book):

Back stitch.

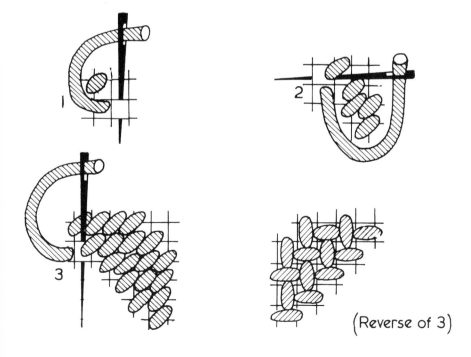

(Reverse of 3)   Basketweave stitch.

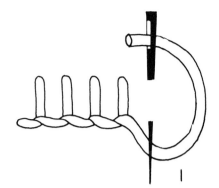

Buttonhole stitch.

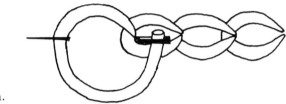

Chainstitch.

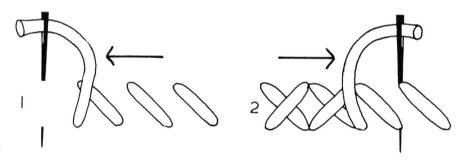

Cross stitch.

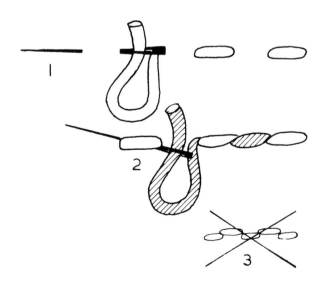

Running stitch.

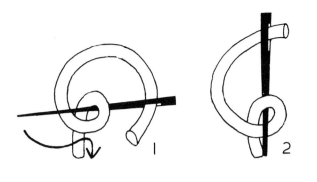

French knot.

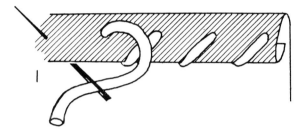

Hemming.

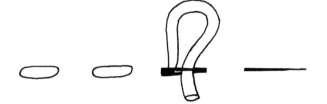

Running stitch.

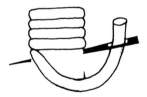

Satin stitch.

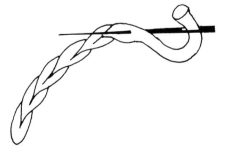

Split stitch.

Stem stitch.

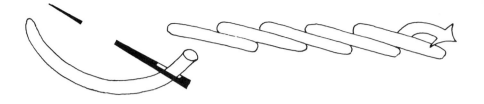

Tent stitch.

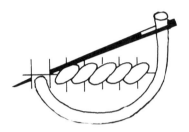

A compensation stitch
(shaded) fills a small ground
area in a style as close as
possible to those stitches
covering the main ground

Compensation stitch.

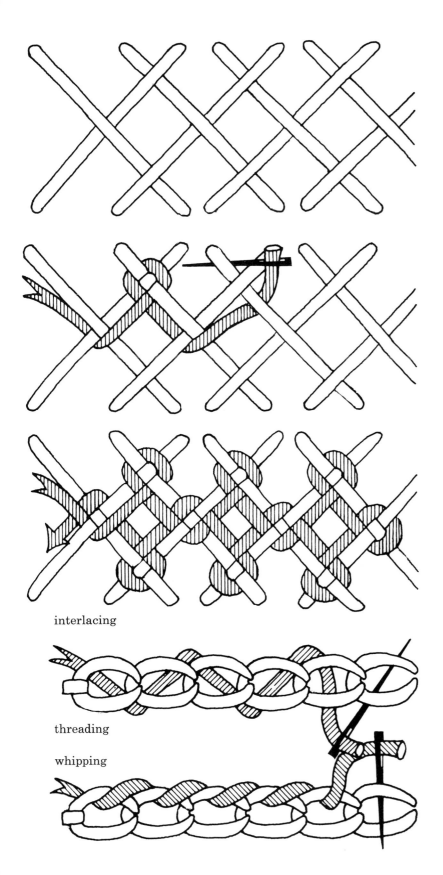

Among the many ways to augment basic stitches once they have been worked are superficial techniques which apart from the beginning and end of each thread, *do not enter the ground fabric*. Three superficial techniques are interlacing, threading and whipping

interlacing

threading

whipping

A stitch can be executed at
whatever angle is most handy.
Left-handed embroiderers
should hold the diagram
in front of a mirror

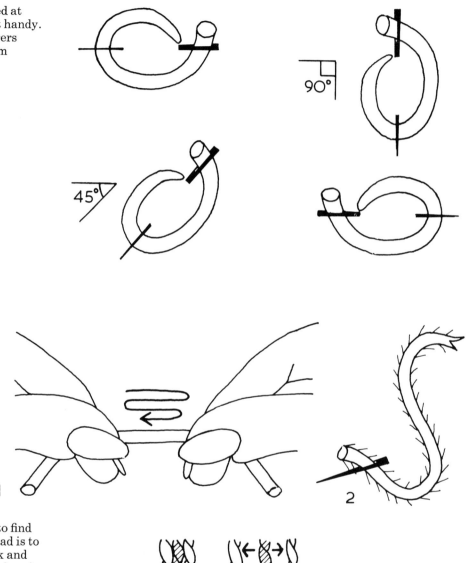

(*Right*) **1** An easy way to find
the nap of woollen thread is to
pull a short length back and
forth close to the skin of one's
upper lip. **2** All wool should be
threaded through the needle
with the hairs running
smoothly back to the ground
fabric. **3** Some wools have
three strands of plied thread.
4 After the nap direction
is determined, the strands
should be separated to give a
fluffier embroidery.

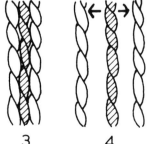

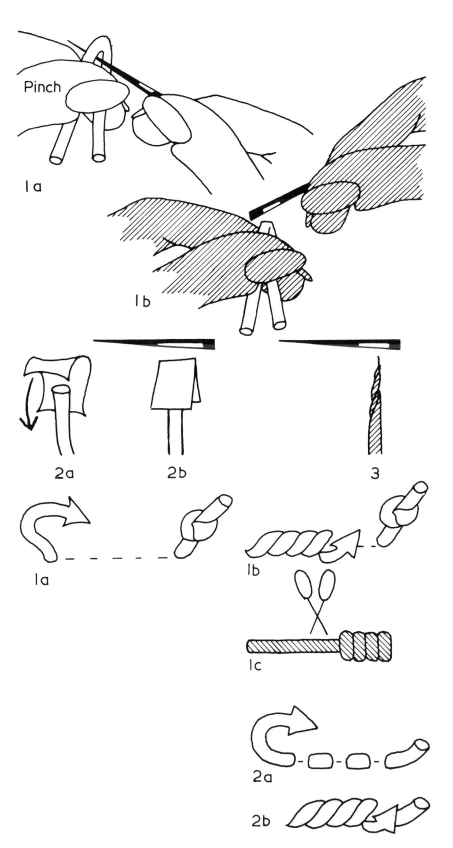

Pinch

1a

1b

2a

2b

3

1a

1b

1c

2a

2b

It is sometimes difficult to get a thick thread through the eye of a needle. Three possible solutions are: **1** The thread should be folded around the point end of a needle and pinched hard as close as possible to the needle (a) before attempting to pass the tight fold that results through the needle's eye (b). **2** The cut end of a length of thread should be placed inside the fold of a piece of paper (a) narrow enough to fit within the length of the needle's eye (b). The paper with thread then passes easily through the eye. **3** The end of the thread can be moistened or twisted firmly before being pushed through the eye

Beginning a new thread should never be done with a permanent knot. Two solutions, both originating away from the start of the embroidery and worked back towards it, are: **1** The end to be secured is temporarily knotted. From the front of the fabric, a long stitch is taken towards the beginning of the embroidered design (a), then sewn normally, catching in the long retaining thread on the wrong side (b). After a few stitches the retaining thread is cut from the reverse (c). **2** Tiny running stitches are worked (a) and then covered by embroidery stitches (b)

Suppliers

A comprehensive selection of all materials (including NEPO and invisible markers and all DMC threads) is available from The Silver Thimble, 33 Gay Street, Bath, Avon BA1 2NT, who have a regularly updated catalogue and a newsletter.

If you are in London and would like to look at embroidery threads and materials, The Royal School of Needlework has a shop in its headquarters at 25 Prince's Gate, London SW7 1QE.

Acknowledgements

I should like to thank my dear friend Joan Hall who helped me stitch many of the pieces in this book. Other embroiderers who helped make the book possible are Elspeth Campbell, Diana May, Lorna Parkin, Brenda Powell, Pat Prowse, Shirley Rowe and Stephanie Teychenné.

Index

Page numbers in italic type
refer to illustrations

Alderson, Chottie, *87*, 99, *100*
Appliqué, 11–18, *11*, *13–18*, *65*, *66*,
  70
Ashmolean Museum, 26, *26*
Assisi work, 19–21, *20*, *21*

Backgammon board, 39–42, *40–2*
Back stitch, 27, *106*, 139, 142,
  142, *143*
Bag, Assisi work, 19–21, *19–21*
Bargello, 22–4, *23–4*, *86*, *87*, 123,
  124
Bargello, freeform, *85*
Basic embroidery survival kit, 7,
  8
Basket, embroidery, 7, *8*, 9–10
Basketweave tent stitch, 64, 69,
  101, 103, *143*, 148
Bedjacket, 34
Beginning a new thread, 149
Birth sampler, *53*
Blackwork, 26–9, *26–9*
Blackwork 'special clutch', 26–9,
  26–9
Blanket cover, machine-stitched,
  90–2, *90–2*
Blocking, 69–71, *71*
Box, couched, 43–6, *43–6*
Broderie anglaise, *30–4*, 31–4, *85*
Broderie anglaise housecoat,
  30–4, *30–4*, *85*
Broderie anglaise, padded, *34*
Buttonhole stitch, *144*

Cable stitch, 135, *136–7*, 137
California-style jacket, *see*
  Patchwork jacket
Camera case, *86*, 116–18, *116*
Canvaswork, *see* Needlepoint
Card embroidery, 35–8, *35–8*
Chainstitch, 12, 39–42, *40–2*, 94,
  142, *144*
Chainstitched games boards,
  39–42, *40–2*
Chessboard, 39–42, *40–2*
Chevron stitch, 135, *136–7*, 137
Christening robe, 134–7, *134*
Christmas cards, 36–7, *37*, 98
Chottie's plaid, *87*, 99, *100*
Circle, cutting a, 10, *10*
Clutch bag, blackwork, 26–9,
  26–9
Compensation stitch, 146

Coton-a-broder, 27
Cotton, stranded, 7, 19, 27, 31, 45,
  126, 128
Cotton, stranded, stripping, 7, 19,
  45
Couched box, 43–6, *43–6*, *86*
Couching, 43–6, *43–6*, *86*, 123
Counted thread, *see* Cross stitch
  and Samplers
Crewel mirror surround, 47–50,
  47–50, *68*
Cross stitch, 19, *67*, *127*, 128, *144*
Cross stitch samplers, 51–9,
  52–9. *67*, 126–9, *127*
Cutting a circle, 10, *10*

Double hemstitch, *74*
Double running stitch, 27, *144*
Drawn thread, *68*, 72, *73*, 74, *74*
Drawn thread tie, *68*, 72–4, *73–4*
Dressmaking, 32, 60–1, *61*, 83–4,
  84, 93, 94, *94*, *101–3*, 139

Equipment, 7, *8*

Felt, 11–18, *11–18*, *20*, 39–42,
  40–2, 43–6, *43–6*, *65*, *66*
Festoon stitch, 114, *114*
Florentine, *see* Bargello
Floss, *see* Cotton, stranded
Fly stitch, 48, *49*
Frames, embroidery, 7, *8*, 31, *45*,
  92, *92*
French knots, 27, *27*, *29*, 48, *82*,
  83, *89*, 98, *98*, *142*, *145*

Games boards, 39–42, *40–42*
Gesner, Conrad, 19

Hardanger tray, 75–7, *75*, *77*
Hardanger work, 77
Hedebo stitch, *80–1*, 81
Hedebo sun visor, 78–81, *78–82*
Hedebo work, *78*, *80*
Hemming, *145*
Hemstitch, *74*
Hoops, embroidery, 7, *8*, 31, 45,
  92, *92*
Housecoat, broderie anglaise,
  30–4, *30–4*

Interlacing, 147
Invisible pen, 7, *8*

Jacket, patchwork, *see*
    Patchwork jacket

Kaftan, *88*, 93–6, *93–6*

Laid and couched work, *see*
    Couching
Leaf stitch, 48, *49*
Lettering, 51, *52*, *82*, 83, *89*, 127–8

Machine-stitched blanket cover,
    90–2, *90–2*
Machine stitching, 90–2, *90–2*,
    116
Markers, 7
Metal thread on a kaftan, *88*,
    93–6, *93*, *95–6*, 125
Miniature figure, *87*
Mirror surround, crewel, 47–50,
    47–50, 68

Nap, of thread, 148
Needlepainting, *96*, 97–8, *98*
Needlepoint, 63–4, *70*, *120*, *123*,
    124
Needlepoint from a child's
    painting, 63–4, *63*, *66*, *70*
Needlepoint on a child's dress,
    87, *100*
Needlepoint tabard, 99, *100*, 101,
    102
Needlepoint waistcoat, *87*, 99,
    100–1, 101
NEPO pen, 7, *8*
Net curtain, *104–6*, 105–6

Patchwork jacket, 107, *108–10*,
    109–11
Pattern darned skirt, 60–2, *60–2*
Pattern darning, 61, *61–2*
Pattern, tracing a, *9*, 27
Pen, 'invisible', 7, *8*
Pin cushion, *130*, 131–3, *132–3*
Pulled thread tissue cover,
    112–15, *112–15*
Pulled thread work, *112*, *114*
Puppets, appliqué, 11–18, *11*,
    13–18, *65*, *66*, *70*

Quilted camera case, *86*, 116–18,
    116–18
Quilting, 27–8, *27–8*, *86*, 116–18,
    116–18
Quilting, Italian, 118, *118*

Raised work, 119

Raised work miniature figure,
    119–25, *120–3*, *124–5*
Running stitch, *145*

Samplers, 51–9, *52–9*, *67*, 126–9,
    127–9
Satin stitch, 27, *27*, *29*, 34, *77*,
    130, 131, *133*, *142*, *145*
Scale, 7
Scissors, 7, *8*
Seam allowance, 7
Self-couching, *123*
Sewing machine, 91–2, *91–2*
Shadow work pincushion, *130*,
    131–3, *132–3*
Skirt, pattern darned, 60–2, *60–2*
Smocking, 134–7, *134–6*
Split stitch, *145*
Stem stitch, 48, *49*, *146*
Stiletto, 33, *34*
Stitch diagrams, *143–6*
Straight stitch, 48, *49*, *96*, *142*
Stranded cotton, 19, 27, 31, 45,
    126, 128
Stranded cotton, stripping, 7, 19,
    45
Stripping, *see* Stranded cotton
Stumpwork, *see* Raised work
Sun visor, Hedebo, 78–81, *78–82*
Suppliers of embroidery
    materials, 147

Tassels, 46, *46*
Tennis dress, *82*, 83–4, *89*
Tent stitch, 64, 69, 101, 103, *143*,
    146
Threading, 149
Threading a needle, 149
Tie, drawn thread, *68*, 72–4, *73–4*
Tracing a pattern, *9*
Tray, hardanger, 75–7, *75*, *77*
Tyler rose stitch, *87*, *120*, *123*
Typewriter cover, Bargello,
    22–5, *22–5*, *86*

Velcro, 25, *25*, 71, *71*

Wedding dress, *138*, 139, *140–1*,
    142
Wedding sampler, *56*
Whipping, 147
Whitework, *see* Broderie
    anglaise, Net curtain project
    and Pincushion project
Woodcuts, 26, *26*

Zip fastener, putting in, 60–1, *61*